OXFORD
UNIVERSITY PRESS

Annette Flavel

Workbook

1 What can we do to help our well-being?

Vocabulary 1

A **Complete the sentences.**

take a picture   ill   curry   travel   ~~patient~~

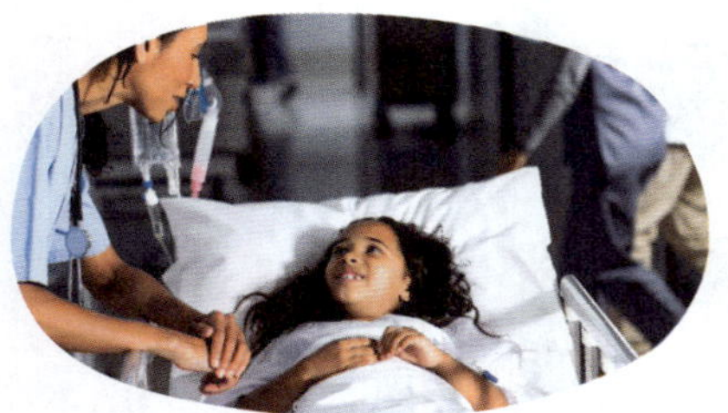

1 The doctor is checking on her ___patient___.

2 Can we have vegetable _____________ for dinner?

3 I don't feel well today. I'm _____________.

4 I like to _____________ around the world.

5 Let's _____________ together.

B **Unscramble the words in parentheses to complete the conversation.**

Ji-hu: I want to try something new. How do you stay [1] active_________ (taciev)?

Briana: I like to swim and do [2] y_____________ (ogya). Both help me feel better when I am [3] s_____________ (seserdts). How about you?

Ji-hu: I do a lot of outdoor sports. Sometimes, I go [4] h_____________ (khingi) in the [5] m_____________ (miotasnun).

Briana: I have an idea. Let's do these activities together!

Grammar

A **Complete the chart.**

Add *-ing*	Double the final letter and add *-ing*	Drop the *-e* and add *-ing*
be → ___being___	run → ___running___	take → ___taking___
cook → ___________	swim → ___________	dance → ___________
go → ___________	stop → ___________	hike → ___________
play → ___________	dig → ___________	smile → ___________

B **Circle the correct option.**

1 He enjoys **cooked** / **(cooking)** with his grandma.

2 I enjoy **swim** / **swimming** in the pool on a sunny day.

3 Alicia goes **running** / **run** every morning. She likes **be** / **being** active.

4 On the weekend, we like **dancing** / **dance** together.

5 I like **go** / **going** to my cousins' house. We have a lot of fun.

C **Complete the sentences. Use the gerund form of the verbs.**

hike   spend   help   ~~play~~   talk

1 They like ___playing___ basketball together after school.

2 ___________ patients is a doctor's job.

3 I enjoy ___________ time with my friends on the weekend.

4 ___________ in the mountains is good exercise.

5 My grandma likes ___________ with her friends on the phone.

1 **A:** Do you like sleeping late on Saturday?

   B: Yes, I do. / No, I don't.

2 **A:** Do they like singing and dancing?

   B: Yes, they do. / No, they don't.

3 **A:** Does he like hiking?

   B: Yes, he does. / No, he doesn't.

4 **A:** Does she enjoy spending time with her grandparents?

   B: Yes, she does. / No, she doesn't.

E Unscramble the questions.

1 hugging / does / help / ? / our emotions / How

   How does hugging help our emotions?

2 singing and dancing / Why / love / do / ? / you

   ____

3 fresh air / ? / feel good / breathing / Why / does

   ____

4 How / doing yoga / ? / help / does / you

   ____

What do you enjoy doing on Saturdays?

A Read the interview. What does Alana do to help her well-being?

Cousin Time!

A student interviews her older cousin about well-being.

Lina: Alana, that was an amazing game! You're really good at playing tennis.

Alana: Hi, Prima! Thank you for coming.

Lina: Can I interview you for my school project?

Alana: Yes, of course. What do you want to know?

Lina: What do you do to help your well-being?

Prima = Cousin

Alana: Well, playing tennis is great for my well-being. I practice a lot.

Lina: What other things do you do to help your well-being?

Alana: I love spending time with my friends. We like dancing together, and sometimes we go hiking. It helps when we're feeling stressed. I also like cooking. Preparing and eating healthy foods makes me feel good.

Lina: What's your favorite food?

Alana: I like vegetable curry. You like my curry, too, don't you?

Lina: I love it! You're a great cook.

Alana: Thank you!

Lina: Why is well-being important to you?

Alana: I want everyone to be happy and healthy.

Lina: Is that why you're studying to be a doctor?

Alana: Yes, exactly! I want all my patients to live long, happy, healthy lives.

Lina: That's a good plan. Does anything else help your well-being?

Alana: I sit and study every day, so I need to make sure I am active, too. I always do my homework, but I take time to do things I enjoy. I have tennis practice four times a week, and I also do yoga on Sunday mornings.

Lina: Thank you for the interview! I think you have a good life now, and I know you will be a great doctor. You care about everyone's well-being. I want to be just like you!

B Underline these words in the text.

hiking   stressed   curry   patients   active   yoga

C Read the sentences. Circle *Fact* or *Opinion*.

1 Lina interviews her cousin for a school project.   Fact   Opinion

2 Alana is studying to be a doctor.   Fact   Opinion

3 Alana's favorite food is vegetable curry.   Fact   Opinion

4 Lina thinks Alana is a great cook.   Fact   Opinion

5 Lina thinks Alana will be a good doctor.   Fact   Opinion

6 Alana goes to tennis practice four times a week.   Fact   Opinion

D Check (✓) the things Alana does to help her well-being.

1 ☐ She plays tennis.

2 ☐ She plays basketball.

3 ☐ She does yoga.

4 ☐ She plays video games.

5 ☐ She spends time with friends.

6 ☐ She cooks healthy meals.

A **Read and choose the correct option.**

B **Two of the three options are correct. Cross out (X) the wrong option.**

1 You can eat these.	**a** broccoli	**b** corn	**c** ~~bone~~
2 These are part of your body.	**a** muscle	**b** bone	**c** beans
3 These are food groups.	**a** vitamins and minerals	**b** grains	**c** protein

A Match the sentences to the pictures.

a

1 I like to lie down in the sun and relax.

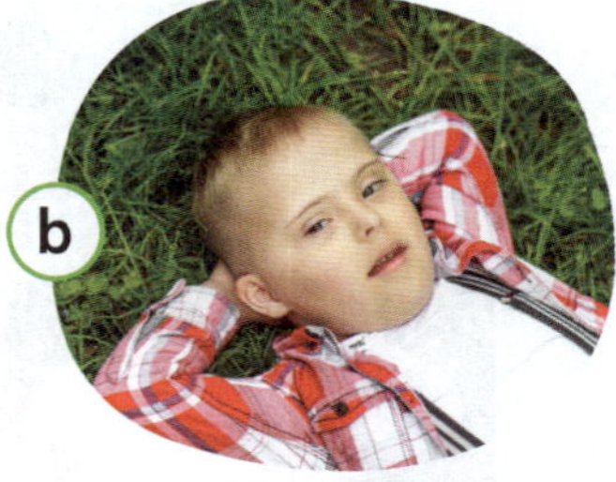

b

2 Don't be scared. You can do it. Be brave!

c

3 Before I draw a picture, I try to imagine it.

d

4 Sometimes, when I can't do what I want, I feel angry.

5 This math test was hard, but I studied a lot!

e

6 What are you worried about?

f

B Circle the correct option.

Avril: I had a math [1] **test** / **imagine** today.

Karim: Really? How was it?

Avril: Before the test, I was [2] **angry** / **worried**. But it was easy!

Karim: That's great! Now you can [3] **relax** / **imagine**.

What do you do to relax?

Writing Study

A **Complete the dialogues with *who*, *what*, *when*, *where*, or *why*.**

1 **A:** _______________________ do you talk to
   when you have a problem?
   B: My mom.

2 **A:** _______________________ do you eat to
   stay healthy?
   B: I eat fruits and vegetables.

3 **A:** _______________________ do you do yoga?
   B: Because it helps me relax.

4 **A:** _______________________ do you play basketball?
   B: In the park.

5 **A:** _______________________ do you wake up in the morning?
   B: At 6:00 a.m.

B **Unscramble the questions.**

1 Where / on weekdays / eat lunch / ? / do you

   ____

2 to talk to / ? / on the phone / do you / Who / like

   ____

3 worried / ? / What / feel / makes you

   ____

4 do you go / to sleep / ? / When / at night

   ____

5 don't / you / eat meat / Why / ?

   ____

C **Write questions with *who*, *what*, *when*, *where*, or *why* in your notebook.
Then ask your partner.**

Who... _______________________   Where... _______________________

What... _______________________   Why... _______________________

When... _______________________

A **Circle the correct option.**

1 Fruits and vegetables have lots of **bones** / **vitamins and minerals** / **mountains** in them.

2 Brenda feels **active** / **protein** / **ill**. She's very tired and warm.

3 Sometimes I'm happy, and sometimes I'm sad. I have many **beans** / **bones** / **emotions**.

4 Ilian has a lot of homework, so he feels **stressed** / **relaxed** / **imagine**.

5 My aunt and I went to a **test** / **curry** / **yoga** class in the park last Saturday.

6 Take some deep breaths and **relax** / **angry** / **muscle**. Everything will be OK.

7 Chicken, eggs, and fish all have a lot of **grains** / **worried** / **protein**.

8 Think of a happy place. What do you **relax** / **imagine** / **hiking**?

B **Complete the sentences. Use the gerund form of the verbs.**

watch   eat   hike   play   sing   swim

1 They enjoy _____________ in the mountains.

2 He doesn't like _____________ in the ocean. He prefers the pool.

3 We like _____________ vegetable curry at that Indian restaurant.

4 My brother and I like _____________ funny cartoons.

5 When I'm sad, I love _____________ happy songs.

6 My sister enjoys _____________ tennis.

Unit 1 and Me

How hard I worked ☆☆☆☆☆   Did I reach my goal?   

One thing I learned is ____.

My goal for Unit 2 is ____.

2 How can we help the well-being of others?

Vocabulary 1

A Match the sentences to the pictures.

1 My little brother likes playing with his friends in kindergarten.

2 Juno enjoys sewing doll clothes.

3 Lila won the karate competition. She's really proud.

4 Can you hand out the worksheets, please?

5 This is a very thin needle.

B Complete the paragraph.

message   bookmark   nursing home   picture book   blanket

Every afternoon, Angela reads a [1] ________________ to her little brother, Allen. They sit under a warm [2] ________________ on the sofa and look at the book together. Next week, they are going to visit their grandfather, Sergio. Grandpa Sergio lives in a [3] ________________ ________________ with other older people because he needs special help. Today, Grandpa Sergio sent them a [4] ________________ . It said, "I can't wait to see you! Bring a book, so we can read together." Angela chose a book to bring, and Allen is going to give Grandpa Sergio a [5] ________________ he made in kindergarten.

A Complete the sentences with *can* or *can't*.

1 He _________________ read well. He likes books about science.

2 She _________________ climb the wall yet, but she's learning.

3 They _________________ play tennis well. They practice a lot!

4 I _________________ play soccer with you today. I'm ill.

B Match the sentence halves.

1 Josie could ride a bike …

2 You couldn't walk …

3 When I was in kindergarten, …

4 My friend couldn't …

5 My sister couldn't drive …

6 Oscar could talk …

a when she was 10.

b sleep last night.

c when he was two.

d when she was seven.

e I couldn't write.

f when you were a baby.

1 Can Vanessa play video games?

Yes, she can. / No, she can't.

2 Can she draw?

Yes, she can. / No, she can't.

3 Can she dance well?

Yes, she can. / No, she can't.

4 Can she sew?

Yes, she can. / No, she can't.

5 Can Sam sew?

Yes, he can. / No, he can't.

6 Can he draw well?

Yes, he can. / No, he can't.

D Complete the dialogues with *can, can't, could,* or *couldn't.*

1 **A:** Two years ago, I _________________ swim.

B: _________________ you swim now?

A: Yes, I _________________ .

2 **A:** _________________ you play the guitar last year?

B: No, I _________________ .

A: _________________ you play the guitar now?

B: No, I _________________ . But I still want to learn!

3 **A:** When my brother was one, he _________________ walk.

B: _________________ he walk now?

A: Yes, he _________________ . He can run and jump, too!

What can you do now? Could you do it two years ago?

A **Read the article. How are the children similar?**

HOW WE HELP

**Helping can make us feel happy.
Here's how some friends around the world help in their communities.**

Luis and his classmates live in Lima, Peru. Every year, they bring books to another school in the neighborhood. They bring storybooks for the older students and picture books for the kindergarten children. They make a bookmark to go with each book. Luis loves handing out new books to the students. Then they all have a reading party. Everyone at the school has a new book to read!

Emma visits her grandfather every week. He lives in a nursing home in Munich, Germany. Every September, Emma and her friends make cards for Grandparents' Day. Some people in the nursing home live far from their grandchildren. Their grandchildren rarely visit them. Emma and her friends make cards for these grandparents, too!

Some of the people in the nursing home can sew well. This week, they are sewing small bags for Emma and her friends. They want to say "thank you" for the cards on Grandparents' Day.

Aiden, his mom, and his sisters Olivia and Isabella live in South Carolina, USA. After school, they sometimes volunteer at an animal shelter. They all like helping the animals. There are some kittens at the shelter now. They don't have a home yet. The kittens enjoy playing, and they get hungry often. Aiden and his sisters give the kittens food. His mom washes their blankets. Then they take photos of the kittens playing. The pictures go on the shelter's website to help the kittens find homes. It feels good to help.

B Underline these words in the text.

picture books   kindergarten   bookmark
handing out   nursing home   sew   blankets

C Circle the correct answer.

1 Who do Luis and his classmates help?   **grandparents** / **animals** / **other children**

2 What do Luis and his friends make?   **blankets** / **bookmarks** / **cards**

3 What do Emma and her friends give the grandparents?   **bags** / **letters** / **cards**

4 What do some grandparents give Emma and her friends?   **hats** / **bags** / **blankets**

5 Where do Aiden and his family help the kittens?   **a shelter** / **a park** / **a school**

6 Who do they go there with?   **Olivia's dad** / **Aiden's mom** / **Luis and his classmates**

D Match to complete the main ideas.

1 Luis and his friends help …   •   with the animals …   •   at the nursing home.

2 Emma and her friends help …   •   with books …   •   at the elementary school.

3 Aiden and his family help …   •   with cards …   •   at the animal shelter.

A Number the pictures to match the sentences.

1 Aunt Teresa is a firefighter.

2 Please fill this pot with water.

3 Jordana can juggle really well.

4 My friends really like making crafts.

 3

B Complete the conversation.

> fit   band   volunteer   crafts   sign up

Ms. Best: Hi! I'm a ¹ ______________ here. Can I help you?

Jim: Yes, thank you. Where can I ² ______________ for the fun run?

Ms. Best: Right here. I can help you.

Jim: Oh, great! I run every afternoon, so I'm ³ ______________ .

Ms. Best: You'll do great! After the fun run, there's a festival. You can listen to the ⁴ ______________ and make some ⁵ ______________ , too.

Jim: Thanks! That sounds like fun!

A Unscramble the words to complete the sentences.

1 My teacher gave me a c _______________ (mpcolenimt).

2 In the morning, I w _______________ (wita) for the bus with my mom.

3 That's an e _______________ (romuneso) dinosaur!

4 I hope I score a g _______________ (oagl) during the game today.

B Circle the correct option.

Caro: We gave our teacher a box of chocolates. It was [1] **wait** / **enormous** / **compliment** .

Jamal: Really? Why?

Caro: To show our [2] **appreciation** / **goal** / **receive** . She's a really good teacher!

Jamal: Was she happy to [3] **wait** / **crafts** / **receive** them?

Caro: Yes, she was. She said, "You are very kind!"

Jamal: That's a great [4] **compliment** / **goal** / **enormous** !

Can you think of a compliment to give someone?

A Read the interview. Label the parts of the interview.

> Ask other useful questions
> Ask *who*, *what*, *when*, *where* or *why* questions

Last week, I interviewed Bin Soula. He participated in a walk-a-thon last weekend.

Ronnie: Hello, Bin! Thank you for talking to me.

Bin: Hello, Ronnie. **1**

Ronnie: What's a walk-a-thon?

Bin: People come to the park on a certain date and walk to raise money. Last week, we raised money for books and supplies for local schools.

Ronnie: How far did you walk?

Bin: Ten kilometers. It's good exercise, and it's good to walk for a reason.

Ronnie: How many people were there? **2**

Bin: About 100 people came. Both children and adults participated.

Ronnie: My friend's dad is blind. Can he do a walk-a-thon?

Bin: Yes, he can. He can bring his guide dog, and a volunteer can help him, too.

Ronnie: Thank you, Bin. I enjoyed talking to you.

B Plan your interview in your notebook. Write some *who*, *what*, *when*, *where*, and *why* questions to ask.

C Use your plan to write your interview in your notebook.

D Check your writing. Use the checkist on page 176 to help you.

A **Complete the sentences.**

> band   firefighter   kindergarten   message   proud   volunteer

1 A ________________ helps to put out fires.

2 My five-year-old brother goes to ________________ .

3 I won the race! I feel so ________________ .

4 My friend sent me a ________________ . She wants to go for a bike ride.

5 Lidia likes to help people. She's going to ________________ at the festival.

6 Hector plays the drums. He wants to join the school ________________ .

B **Complete the sentences with *can*, *can't*, *could*, or *couldn't*.**

1 I ________________ juggle well at first. But now I ________________ juggle three balls.

2 This is an amazing picture. You ________________ draw really well!

3 **A:** ________________ you sew last year?

B: No, I ________________ . But now I ________________ sew a little.

4 **A:** ________________ you swim?

B: Yes, I ________________ . I really enjoy swimming

Unit 2 and Me

How hard I worked ☆☆☆☆☆   Did I reach my goal? ☺ ☺ ☹

One thing I learned is ____ .

My goal for Unit 3 is ____ .

3 How can we improve our well-being?

A **Complete the sentences.**

> barn   rainbow   vacation   field

1 Wow! Do you see the _____________ in the sky?

2 Did you go to the beach during your _____________?

3 The horses and cows sleep in the _____________ .

4 The animals run in the grass in the _____________ .

B **Unscramble the words to complete the sentences.**

1 Yum! This pizza has o_____________ (onnio) and g_____________ (icgarl).

2 The r_____________ (rsteoor) is so noisy in the morning.

3 Please cut the c_____________ (cuumebrc) for the salad.

4 That big purple vegetable is an e_____________ (eplaggnt).

5 Look at the big black and yellow s_____________ (uswernflo)!

Where did you go on your last vacation?

A Complete the chart.

Adjectives that end in *-ing*		Adjectives that end in *-ed*
boring	**1**	bored
2		excited
tiring	**3**	
4		surprised
interesting	**5**	
6		amazed

B Complete the sentences with the correct words.

bored / **boring**

1 I'm really _______________ .

2 This book is _______________ .

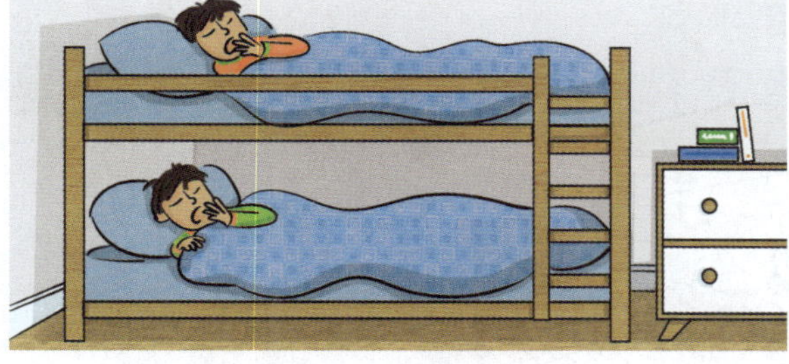

tired / **tiring**

3 Najib and Omar were _______________ .

4 The day was very _______________ .

excited / **exciting**

5 This ride looks _______________ .

6 We are so _______________ !

surprised / **surprising**

7 Leo's birthday present was _______________ .

8 Leo was _______________ .

 Unscramble the questions and answers to make dialogues.

1 A: the roosters / ? / Are / tired   A: _______________________________

   B: not / . / No, / they're   B: _______________________________

2 A: that book / ? / Is / interesting   A: _______________________________

   B: is / it / . / Yes,   B: _______________________________

3 A: you / Are / ? / surprised   A: _______________________________

   B: Yes, / am / . / I   B: _______________________________

4 A: boring / ? / Is / farm / the   A: _______________________________

   B: it's / . / No, / interesting   B: _______________________________

D **Circle the correct adjectives to complete the conversation.**

Kristen: Was your canoe trip [1] **exciting** / **excited** ?

Luna: Yes, it was. I was really [2] **exciting** / **excited**. But the insects in the woods were really [3] **annoying** / **annoyed**. What did you do last weekend?

Kristen: I read a book about karate. It was really [4] **interesting** / **interested**. But then I watched a movie about the story.

Luna: Was it good?

Kristen: No, it was [5] **bored** / **boring**. I was so [6] **bored** / **boring** that I fell asleep!

Luna: I hope the rest of your weekend was good.

Kristen: Oh, yes. On Sunday, my family went hiking in the mountains. It was a [7] **tired** / **tiring** hike. But there were no insects!

Was your weekend interesting or boring? Why?

A 🔧 **Look at the title and the pictures. Circle the best prediction.**

1 What's the story about?

    a Two girls at school   **b** Two girls playing video games   **c** Two girls on a trip to the city

B **Read the story. Then check your prediction from A.**

The Garden

Two twins, Jeanne and Louise, lived on a farm near Marigot in the south of Haiti. On their birthday, their Uncle Junior and Aunt Josie called …

"Happy birthday!" they said. "We have a surprise for you. We're driving to visit you. See you soon."

Jeanne and Louise were surprised and excited.

When their aunt and uncle arrived, they asked the twins, "Would you like to come to Jacmel with us? We can have fun in the city together."

The girls looked at their mom and dad. "Can we go? Please?"

"Yes," they replied. The twins cheered.

Later that day, the twins left with their aunt and uncle. "Bye, Mom! Bye, Dad!" they said. They looked out the window and saw green fields. Then they saw the city. The trip to Jacmel wasn't tiring at all. It was exciting!

The next morning, Uncle Junior cooked eggs for breakfast. He added garlic and onions to them. "I grew the garlic and onions," he said.

"How?" asked Louise, surprised. "You don't have a garden. You live in the city." Uncle Junior smiled. "Let's take a walk," he said.

Soon, they saw a large garden. "It's a community garden," Uncle Junior said. "We all share it. I grow garlic, onions, and eggplants over here!" he said proudly. "And my friend grows cucumbers over there." He pointed. The garden was green and beautiful. The twins were amazed!

Later, they saw a little boy holding seeds in his hands. He looked confused.

"Hi, I'm Jeanne. What's wrong?"

"Well," the boy said, "I want to plant these, but I don't know how. They're sunflowers."

"We can help you," said Louise.

"Really? I'm so excited." said the boy.

"Thank you for helping me!" said the boy. "Now the garden will be even more amazing."

"You're welcome!" said Jeanne.

"Thank you for being good helpers," said Aunt Josie. "Let's go have lunch. I picked lots of vegetables to make legume."

"Mmm, yummy! Let's go!" said Louise.

legume = vegetable stew

C **Underline these words in the text.**

fields   garlic   onions   eggplants   cucumbers   sunflowers

D **Check your prediction. Were you right?**

◯ Yes   ◯ No

E **Read and circle the correct answer.**

1 Whose birthday was it?

  a Aunt Josie   **b** Jeanne and Louise   **c** Uncle Junior

2 Where do Aunt Josie and Uncle Junior live?

  a in Jacmel   **b** near Marigot   **c** in Sunflower City

3 What does Uncle Junior grow in the garden?

  a garlic, onions, and eggplant   **b** tomatoes and cucumbers   **c** sunflowers

4 What does the little boy want to plant?

  a eggplants   **b** onions   **c** sunflowers

F **Read and write _True_ or _False_.**

1 Uncle Junior and Aunt Josie bought plane tickets for the twins.   __________

2 The twins visited their aunt and uncle in Port-au-Prince.   __________

3 Uncle Junior made pancakes for breakfast.   __________

4 The twins and their aunt and uncle walked to a community garden.   __________

5 The twins helped the little boy plant seeds.   __________

A **Unscramble the words to complete the sentences.**

1 I can't r ___________ (membrree) that girl's name. What is it?

2 We're going on the boat. Put on your l ___________ (lfei vset).

3 It's windy today. I want to fly my new k ___________ (teik).

4 Do you have your s ___________ (wumstisi)? We can go to the pool.

B **Look at A. Number the pictures to match the sentences.**

C **Complete the conversation.**

paddleboats   ice skating   rollerblading   skateboard

Mom: What should we do this afternoon?

Jane: Look! There are canoes and ¹ ___________ over there.
We can go on a boat ride.

Dad: That's a great idea!

Andy: I don't know, Dad. There's a sign for a skate park, and
I brought my ² ___________ with me.

Jane: Really? Can I go ³ ___________ there?

Mom: Sure, you can. Let's all go to the skate park!

Dad: Let's come back in winter, so we can go ⁴ ___________ !

A Follow the path. Number the sentences in order.

☐ It takes you to the waterfall.

☐ There are smooth rocks near the water.

☐ The hiking trail starts at the parking lot.

☐ There are rough rocks along the way.

B Complete the sentences.

smooth   notice   peaceful   rough   trail   waterfall

1 Ouch! The rocks are ______________ . Be careful!

2 Did you ______________ the different colors in the water?

3 The forest is so quiet and ______________ .

4 Walk on the ______________ . You don't want to get lost!

5 Look at this ______________ stone from the river.

6 Do you hear the water? We're close to the ______________ .

What is the most peaceful place you know?

A Make compound nouns. Use one word from each box.

| fire   sand   sun <br> sword   rain   water | drop   castle   fall <br> fish   flower   fly |

B Complete the sentences with compound nouns from **A**.

1 A ______________ is a big, beautiful, yellow plant.

2 The water in a ______________ starts up high and moves down.

3 You can build a ______________ at the beach.

4 A ______________ lights up at night in the summer.

5 A ______________ swims in the ocean.

6 I tried to catch a ______________ in my hand.

C Choose three compound nouns. Write sentences with them in your notebook. 

3 Unit Review

A Two of the three options are correct. Cross out (*X*) the wrong option.

1 **A rock can feel like this.**　　　　　　　a rough　　b smooth　　c notice

2 **You can put these in a salad.**　　　　a cucumber　　b field　　c onion

3 **Wear these when you play in the water.**　a life vest　　b swimsuit　　c kite

4 **Do these activities for fun.**　　　　　a rollerblade　　b ice skate　　c eggplant

5 **You can see these outside.**　　　　　a remember　　b rainbow　　c waterfall

6 **You can find these on a farm.**　　　　a rooster　　b smooth　　c barn

B Complete the dialogues with the correct words.

1 **tiring / tired**

A: How was your train ride to Istanbul?

B: It was long and ______________ .
　I'm ______________ .

2 **exciting / excited**

A: Will you sing in the concert?

B: Yes, I'm really ______________ .

A: That's so ______________ !

3 **amazing / amazed**

A: Did you see Angel Falls?

B: Yes, they were ______________ .
　I was ______________ .

Unit 3 and Me

How hard I worked ☆☆☆☆☆　　Did I reach my goal?   

One thing I learned is ____ .

My goal for Unit 4 is ____ .

Vocabulary 1

A Circle the correct option.

1 This year, I'm in third grade in
bucket / **materials** / **elementary school** .

2 I love sitting under a tree with lots of
deep / **shade** / **wide** .

3 You need **buckets** / **materials** / **shade**
to work in the garden.

4 Can you please hold the sapling
deep / **wide** / **straight** ?

B Unscramble the words in parentheses to complete the sentences.

1 To plant a s______________ (pigsaln), first
we need to dig a h______________ (lohe).

2 It should be d______________ (eped),
w______________ (dwie), and big enough
for the plant.

3 I'm putting soil around the plant with this
s______________ (vesohl).

4 Now, let's water it with the water in this
b______________ (ucbkte).

4 Grammar

A **Match the sentence halves.**

1 When I visit my grandma, …

a he can cool off.

2 If he sits in the shade, …

b I help her in the garden.

3 When she plants the saplings, …

c we can plant these seeds.

4 If they bring us that bag of soil, …

d she plants them straight.

B **Complete the sentences with *if* or *when* and the correct form of the verbs in parentheses.**

1 _____________ he works hard in the garden, he _____________ (feel) tired.

2 _____________ I'm not outside, I _____________ (not wear) boots and gloves.

3 _____________ they cooperate, they _____________ (work) together well.

4 _____________ we don't plant trees, the birds _____________ (not have) homes.

5 _____________ you use the shovel, _____________ (hold) it tightly.

> What does he do   What do you do   What does she do   What do they do
> in the shade   with a shovel   deep, wide hole   the plants

1 **A:** _______________________ if the soil is very dry?

B: She waters _______________________ .

2 **A:** _______________________ when they need a hole?

B: They dig one _______________________ .

3 **A:** _______________________ when it's hot outside?

B: He sits _______________________ .

4 **A:** _______________________ if you have to plant a sapling?

B: You dig a _______________________ .

D **Unscramble the questions.**

1 when you / ? / don't have materials / you do / What do

____

2 if the hole / What do / ? / isn't deep / they do

____

3 he do/ when the bucket / What does / ? / is empty

____

4 at the elementary school / she do / ? / if there's no garden / What does

____

E **Look at D. Number the pictures.**

When you need help, what do you do?

A **Read the report. What are Bayan and her family doing?**

Beach News

Luca Taylor is a volunteer leader. He's helping at Manly Beach for Clean Up Australia Day. He wrote this report to share with the community.

This Saturday, volunteers gathered all over the country for national Clean Up Australia Day. This enormous event is in March every year, and it's something every Australian does at least once. Thousands went to public parks, beaches, and to the sides of roads to pick up trash and make Australia cleaner for everyone.

I'm here with Bayan at the local park in front of Manly Beach.

"Bayan, how old are you?" I asked.

"I'm nine," said Bayan.

"How do you feel about being here today?"

"I'm excited!" said Bayan. "It's my first time at Clean Up Australia Day. I'm looking forward to using my new gloves and cleaning up the beach! Manly Beach is my favorite."

Bayan and her family participated in the clean-up. Bayan's classmates and their families helped, too! There were over 50 people from her school at the clean-up. All together, there were over 200 people helping!

The volunteer leaders had materials to share. First, volunteers gave Bayan's mom a map and some trash bags. Next, Dad got the bucket and shovel from the car. Then, Aunt Alinta checked that everyone had hats, sunscreen, and water. After that, Bayan's little brother Monti got a trash picker, a special long stick with claws at the end for picking up trash. The family was ready!

Finally, they heard the starting whistle, and they worked and worked. At one point, Monti saw some classmates from his elementary school who were also at the event. He said hello to them.

"If we find plastic, cans, or glass bottles, we put them in the recycling bags. If we find other things, we put them in the trash bags. If we find something heavy, we pick it up with the shovel and put it in the bucket," Monti's mom explained. "The trash goes to a landfill, which is a deep, wide hole in the ground. The recycling goes to the recycling center."

"And the heavy things?"

"Well, we give them to the volunteers. Then they decide what is best to do with them."

They picked up trash for four hours. "We're tired, but we're happy," said Aunt Alinta. "Together, we can clean up a huge area that alone seems very hard. We can get a lot more done when we work together. Now we can rest in the shade and know we helped a little bit."

Almost one million volunteers participated in the clean-up day in 12,000 places around the country. That's a lot of clean-up and a lot of cooperation!

B **Underline these words in the text.**

> materials   bucket   shovel   elementary school   deep   wide   shade

C **Match the questions and answers.**

1 Who is Bayan collecting trash with?

2 Where are Bayan and her family collecting trash?

3 What materials do they use?

4 Why are there different kinds of trash bags?

5 How many people participated in the Manly Beach clean up?

a Because they want to separate the trash.

b They use gloves, bags, trash pickers, buckets, and shovels.

c More than 200 people participated.

d She's collecting trash with her mom, dad, brother, and aunt.

e They're at the local park and beach.

D **Number the events in order. Then complete the sentences.**

> Next   First   Then   Finally

☐ _________________ , they get materials, like a map and a trash bag.

☐ _________________ , someone blows a whistle, and the volunteers start cleaning up.

[1] _________________ , they find their local park, beach, or road location.

☐ _________________ , everyone gathers at a meeting point.

A Circle the correct option.

1 Hi! Welcome to my garden. I'm a **gardener** / **mayor** / **carpenter**.

2 Today, I'm going to plant **posters** / **tools** / **wildflowers**.

3 I have **a poster** / **an idea** / **a gardener**!

4 Let's put a **bird feeder** / **mayor** / **tool** in our yard, so birds visit it.

5 I make things with wood. I'm a **gardener** / **carpenter** / **mayor**. Today, I'm making a chair.

6 I'm going to use my **wildflowers** / **posters** / **tools** to make it.

B Complete the texts.

poster   tools   mayor   ideas

1 I can't find my hammer. If you see my ________________, please bring them here.

2 Where is the ________________? She's late for her interview. We're going to talk about the new project to plant more trees in our town.

3 This ________________ shows pictures of many different birds and their names.

4 Do you have any good ________________ for our science project?

4 Vocabulary 3

A Check (✓) the correct option.

1 I love my family and friends. They bring me ….

☐ gymnasium ☐ happiness ☐ fold

2 The teacher asked us to … the paper in half.

☐ fold ☐ crane ☐ principal

3 The … is in charge of the school.

☐ nursing home ☐ principal ☐ happiness

4 A … is a bird with very long legs. It can fly very well.

☐ principal ☐ gymnasium ☐ crane

5 Our team practiced basketball in the school ….

☐ happiness ☐ gymnasium ☐ crane

6 On Saturdays, we visit my grandma. She lives in a ….

☐ principal ☐ gymnasium ☐ nursing home

B Complete the dialogue.

nursing home   principal   gymnasium   happiness

Alison: Did you hear what the [1] ________________ said at school today?

Teri: No, I didn't. What did she say?

Alison: Our school is going to volunteer at a [2] ________________ to help older people.

Teri: That's so nice! We can bring them extra smiles and [3] ________________ .

Alison: Exactly. There's a meeting in the [4] ________________ tomorrow after school.

Teri: Great! Let's go together.

Do you know how to fold a crane?

A **Match the sentence halves.**

1 We want to learn woodworking with a carpenter …

a because they want to help the Earth.

2 He got a book about origami from the library …

b because we want them to come to our garden.

3 They want to plant a garden …

c because he wants to make interesting animals and shapes.

4 My dad and I made a butterfly feeder …

d because we like making things.

5 Many people are planting trees for Earth Day …

e because they love wildflowers.

B **Write as complete sentences.**

1 Why is she folding paper? / Because she wants to make a paper crane.

<u>She is folding paper because she wants to make a paper crane.</u>

2 Why are they using tools? / Because they want to make a bird house.

____

3 Why are you building a bird house? / Because I want birds to come and visit.

____

4 Why are you planting a garden? / Because we like fresh vegetables.

____

5 Why is he making a card? / Because it's his sister's birthday.

____

C **Write three *why* questions in your notebook. Then write complete answers with *because*.**

<u>Why…</u>   <u>Because…</u>
<u>Why…</u>   <u>Because…</u>
<u>Why…</u>   <u>Because…</u>

A **Unscramble the words in parentheses to complete the sentences.**

1 Please bring me a b________________ (tcubek) of water. I need
to water the s________________ (nsalipg) here and those
w________________ (owflsierldw) over there.

2 I'm making a b________________ (drib dreefe). I need
special t________________ (losot) to cut the wood in a
s________________ (ttasrihg) line.

3 The m________________ (yomra) is in charge of the city.
He's visiting different places. Today, he's visiting students and
teachers at an e________________ s________________
(ytelmnaerey hlosoc).

4 Watch out! There's a d________________ (eped)
h________________ (leho) in front of you. Let's get a
s________________ (esovlh) and fill it up.

B **Unscramble the sentences.**

1 If people want / pick up trash / to clean up their town, / . / they can

____

2 want to relax, / . / When I / of a big tree / I sit in the shade

____

3 we have to / be happy, too / ! / If we want / happiness for others,

____

4 to plant a tree, / . / he digs a hole / deep and wide / When he wants

____

Unit 4 and Me

How hard I worked ☆☆☆☆☆　Did I reach my goal?   

One thing I learned is ____.

My goal for Unit 5 is ____.

Vocabulary 1

A Complete the sentences.

> stilts   designer   puppeteers   create   puppet   control

1 Luisa is drawing how the puppet will look and work. She's a ________________ .

2 She likes to ________________ new characters.

3 Look at her draw this amazing ________________ !

4 The people moving the puppet's body are the ________________ .

5 One person is walking on ________________ inside the body.

6 Two people outside ________________ the movement of the head and tail.

B Circle the correct option.

1 He is on **a journey** / **a designer** / **stilts** through the mountains.

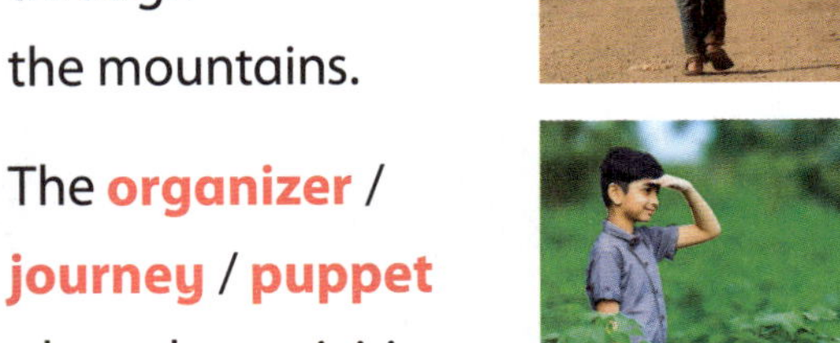

2 It's not safe for me to be in my country. I'm **a designer** / **a refugee** / **an organizer** .

3 The **organizer** / **journey** / **puppet** plans the activities.

4 Can you help me **control** / **search for** / **create** my dog?

What kinds of things do you like to create?

A **Complete the sentences. Use the past continuous form of the verbs in parentheses.**

Yesterday, …

1 She ___was reading___ an exciting book. (read)
2 She _______________ cartoons on TV. (not watch)

3 They _______________ with puppets. (play)
4 They _______________ homework. (not do)

5 He _______________ a burger. (eat)
6 He _______________ curry. (not cook)

7 The boys _______________ . (draw)
8 They _______________ . (not run)

9 They _______________ (create) puppets.
10 They _______________ (not play) board games.

 Look, read, and check (✓).

1 Was the puppet moving in the show yesterday?

☐ Yes, it was. ☐ No, it wasn't.

2 Was the girl crying last night?

☐ Yes, she was. ☐ No, she wasn't.

3 Were the dogs sleeping in the morning?

☐ Yes, they were. ☐ No, they weren't.

4 Were the boys laughing this afternoon?

☐ Yes, they were. ☐ No, they weren't.

 Complete the dialogues.

1 A: What ______________ the boys ______________ last Saturday? (do)

B: They ___________________ with remote control cars.

2 A: What ______________ the girls ______________? (do)

B: They ___________________.

3 A: What ______________ the squirrel ______________? (eat)

B: It ______________ an apple.

4 A: What ______________ the children ______________ to? (listen)

B: They ___________________ to music.

A Read the website article. What kind of event is the article about?

A Show Made by Many

What were you doing on Saturday? A group of children and library volunteers were putting on a puppet show at the library.

Dara's mom is a librarian. She works at a big library in Manila in the Philippines.

One day, Dara went to work with her mom. "We have a lot of grownups at the library," Dara's mom said, "but we want more children to come. Children can have their own library cards, too."

"What are you going to do?" Dara asked.

"Well, we planned some special events," her mom said. "Today, there is a puppet show! I am the organizer."

Dara smiled. "I love puppets! The other kids will, too. What a great idea, Mom!"

"We needed lots of help from the community for the puppet show," said her mom.

Odesa and Jose

Odesa can sew very well. She made curtains for the set. Odesa's husband, Jose, is a carpenter. He created the set out of wood.

Gloria

Gloria is a good writer. She wrote the script for the play.

Mr. Bautista and Tala

Mr. Bautista was the puppet maker. His daughter Tala graduated from art school. She was the puppet designer. Mr. Bautista and Tala were the puppeteers, too. They controlled the puppets in the show.

Many families came to see the puppet show. They were very excited. The show was wonderful. The children clapped and cheered. Afterwards, some of the children signed up for new library cards. The librarians were happy. The puppet show helped them reach their goal!

B Underline these words in the text.

organizer   puppets   created   designer   puppeteers   controlled

C Read and circle *True* or *False*.

1 Dara and her mom are puppeteers.	True	False
2 Dara's mom works at a library.	True	False
3 Everyone uses their different skills to help out.	True	False
4 Mr. Bautista is the puppet show organizer.	True	False
5 No one signs up for a library card.	True	False

D Read the sentences in each box. Write *MI* (main idea) or *D* (detail).

1 The library had a problem. _____

2 They wanted more children to have library cards. _____

3 They wanted families to know how to get library cards. _____

4 Mr. Bautista made the puppets. _____

5 Gloria wrote a script. _____

6 The group cooperated to make the puppet show. _____

7 Many families came to see the show. _____

8 The puppet show was a success. _____

9 Some of the children got library cards. _____

A Write *True* if the sentence is true. Correct the false sentences.

1 A train goes through a ~~pup~~ to get to the other side.   tunnel

2 A **meerkat** is a wild animal that lives in southern Africa. ______

3 A baby meerkat is called a **cobra**. ______

4 We **guard** when we play a game. ______

5 The tiger jumps to **attack** the bird. ______

B Complete the text.

attack   calls   cobras   guards   ~~meerkats~~   take turns   tunnel

In the wild, ¹ __meerkats__ face many dangers. Some animals might ² ______
them. Snakes, such as ³ ______, eat meerkats. To be safe, one meerkat
⁴ ______ the group at all times. If that meerkat sees danger, it ⁵ ______
to the others in a loud voice. If the other meerkats hear the call, they hide in
a ⁶ ______ until it is safe again.

When do you and your friends take turns?

A **Read and match.**

1 This team member helps everyone work together.

2 This team member brings supplies, like tape and scissors.

3 This team member watches the clock.

4 This team member writes down the ideas.

B **Complete the conversation.**

captain   pretend   obstacle course   timekeeper

Juan: Look! The first team is doing the ¹ _______________ . It looks hard!

Olga: Do you see that girl in front? I think she's the ² _______________ of the team.

Juan: There's the ³ _______________ . He's keeping track of the team's time.

Olga: Oh! Do you see that little boy? He doesn't want to cross the bridge.

Juan: He looks afraid. When I'm afraid, I ⁴ _______________ to be a brave animal.

A **Read the play about helping refugees. Label the parts of the play.**

what characters say   what characters do   list of characters   title

1

2

3

4

A Good Idea

Characters: Jeanne   Leah   Henry

Leah and Henry are sitting together in the classroom before school. Jeanne walks in.

Jeanne: Hi! What are you doing?

Leah: We're trying to think of an event to help refugees in our school meet people outside of class.

Henry: I want to do a fun run or a walk-a-thon.

Leah: I want to do something inside, like a concert or a games night.

Jeanne: Why don't we ask the refugees what they like to do.

Leah and Henry look at each other and smile.

Henry: Great idea!

Leah: Excellent idea! Let's ask everyone we know.

B **Plan your play in your notebook. Organize your ideas using the mind map.**

characters

setting

title

what characters say

what characters do

C **Now write your play in your notebook.**

D **Check your writing. Use the checklist on page 176 to help you.**

A Three of the four options are correct. Cross out (*X*) the wrong option.

1 **People:**	a organizer	b refugee	c ~~stilts~~	d puppeteer
2 **Action words:**	a puppet	b control	c create	d search
3 **Animals:**	a meerkat	b cobra	c pup	d take turns
4 **Nouns:**	a obstacle course	b pretend	c captain	d manager
5 **Team members:**	a leader	b scribe	c timekeeper	d tunnel

B Complete the questions and answers with the past continuous form of the verbs in parentheses.

1 **A:** What _______________ the meerkats _______________ (do)?

   B: They _______________ (not sleep).
   They _______________ (guard) against cobras.

2 **A:** What _______________ the puppeteer _______________ (do)?

   B: She _______________ (control) the puppet.

3 **A:** What _______________ the children _______________ (do)?

   B: They _______________ (plan) an obstacle course.

4 **A:** What _______________ the scribe _______________?

   B: She _______________ (not create) the design.
   She _______________ (take) notes.

Unit 5 and Me

How hard I worked ☆☆☆☆☆   Did I reach my goal?    

One thing I learned is ____.

My goal for Unit 6 is ____.

Vocabulary 1

A **Read and check (✓) the correct option.**

1 Spinach is green and healthy.

2 The school fair starts at 2 p.m.

3 Please put some water in this cup.

4 He does research online for his school projects.

B **Complete the sentences.**

> hydroponic   introduce   liter   pests   shortage   sprouted

1 Let me _______________ you. Bernarda, this is Ana. Ana, this is Bernarda.

2 There's a _______________ of water this summer, so we need to use less.

3 The bugs are eating your plants. They are _______________.

4 There are about four glasses of water in a _______________.

5 _______________ vegetables don't need soil. They just need water.

6 When you put the little _______________ seeds in the soil, they grow.

A Circle the action in the simple past. Underline the action in the past continuous.

1 Cecil <u>was working</u> in the garden when it (started) to rain.

2 Fareed was planting more seeds when he saw the first hydroponic tomato.

3 Sophie was picking the spinach when she noticed some pests on the leaves.

4 When the school fair started, we were waiting outside.

B Complete the sentences with the correct form of the verbs in parentheses.

1 Jamilla ____was filling____ (fill) her cup with water when the phone ____rang____ (ring).

2 I ________________ (talk) online with my project team when my mom ________________ (bring) me a snack.

3 I ________________ (research) hydroponics when my friend ________________ (come) over to help.

4 We ________________ (talk) in the garden when we ________________ (see) the pests on the plants.

5 Kenya ________________ (mix) the plant food with water when Allen ________________ (introduce) himself.

C Rewrite the sentences in your notebook. Put the *when* clause first. 

D Look and complete the dialogues with *was*, *were*, *wasn't*, or *weren't*.

1 **A:** _____________________ Mom using the computer?

   B: No, she _____________________ .

2 **A:** _____________________ Dad cooking dinner?

   B: Yes, he _____________________ .

3 **A:** _____________________ the children doing their homework?

   B: No, they _____________________ .

4 **A:** _____________________ Mom and the children watching TV?

   B: Yes, they _____________________ .

5 **A:** _____________________ Grandma carrying a shopping bag?

   B: Yes, she _____________________ .

E Look at **D**. Underline the past continuous.

F Unscramble the questions.

1 What / started / when / were / ? / doing / you / the movie

____

2 were / you / ? / arrived / doing / What / when the teacher

____

3 you / saw / when / doing / What / the pests / were / you / ?

____

A Read the online project report. What project did the team choose?

Online Project: Composting to Reduce Waste 

SEOUL, SOUTH KOREA

BEIRUT, LEBANON

NARI

Our teacher in Korea knows a teacher in Lebanon. Our classes were part of an interesting project called "Let's Save the Planet." We worked together to find a way to make less waste. My partner Hwan and I met with our Lebanese friends online. Our team met every week. First, we shared ideas. Then we did research. Finally, we posted information to our online scrapbook.

HWAN

On the first day, Nari and I introduced ourselves to Hassan and Lara. We talked about food waste in our countries and in other countries around the world. What project could our team do? We went online and learned about composting. Composting turns plant waste into soil with the help of pests. The pests eat the leaves and old vegetables and turn them to soil. We thought it was a good idea, but we needed more information.

HASSAN

We decided on a composting project. First, I asked my Aunt Sara about composting. I visited her garden, and then we all researched online. If you put plants, old vegetables, and fruit in a box outside, they become compost. You have to turn the compost over with a shovel to give it air. The compost makes the soil healthier. Then, later, you can use the soil.

LARA

Our team was great. Nari was the team captain. She gave us instructions and was a good organizer. I am good at art on the computer, so I made the diagrams. Hwan and Hassan are good writers. They posted the information on the online scrapbook. It was exciting to work on a project to help the planet and make new friends, too!

How to Compost

1 Choose a plastic, wood, or wire compost box.
2 Put a layer of dry brown material and a layer of green material (fresh fruit, vegetables, plants) in the compost box.
3 Add some soil and a liter of water.
4 Use a shovel to turn the compost. This gives it air.
5 Wait until it all becomes soil.
6 Use the soil in your garden.
7 Don't put oil, dairy, or meat in the compost box.

B **Underline these words in the text.**

introduced   pests   researched   liter

C **Circle the correct answer.**

1 Where do the children live?
   a South Korea and Lebanon   b China and Mexico   c Egypt and Brazil
2 Where do they meet?
   a in person   b online   c at school
3 What is their project about?
   a saving electricity   b reducing food waste   c recycling
4 How do they get information for their project?
   a research online and do an interview
   b find a book and phone a friend
   c watch a nature show on TV and take notes
5 What do they use to make their online project?
   a diagrams and writing   b video and pictures   c podcasts and stickers

D **Look at the diagram and instructions at the top of the page. Complete the chart.**

cheese   bananas   chicken   dry grass
dry leaves   fresh grass   lettuce   oil   spinach

Green Layer	Brown Layer	Can't Compost

A Unscramble the words in parentheses to complete the sentences.

1 I enjoy f______________ (fiinhsg) on the weekend.

2 Let's go to the m______________ (miarne prka).

3 The o______________ (oopcuts) lives in the ocean.

4 The internet reaches almost every part of the world. It's g______________ (blalog).

B Complete the sentences.

> oxygen   agreement   whale   net

1 People, animals, and birds breathe ______________.

2 That's not a big fish. It's a ______________!

3 Can you catch fish with a ______________?

4 Our ______________ was to finish the project by Monday.

C Look at **B**. Number the pictures.

A Check (✓) the correct option.

1 If you have a ______________ , see a doctor.

☐ disease   ☐ vaccine   ☐ needle

2 The nurse put the ______________ in my arm.

☐ cough   ☐ virus   ☐ needle

3 A ______________ travels through the air.

☐ needle   ☐ vaccine   ☐ virus

4 This ______________ stops you from becoming ill.

☐ vaccine   ☐ virus   ☐ smallpox

5 Years ago, many people became ill and died from ______________ .

☐ vaccine   ☐ cough   ☐ smallpox

6 Please cover your mouth when you ______________ !

☐ needle   ☐ cough   ☐ vaccine

B Look at A. Number the pictures to match the sentences.

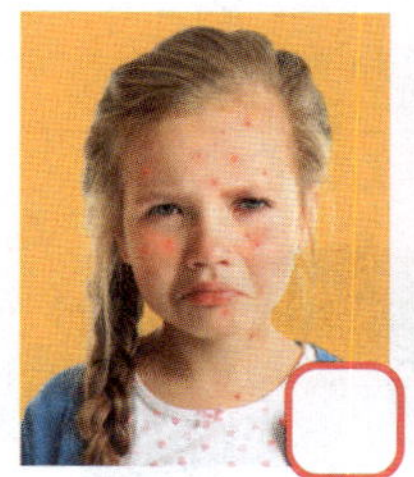 ☐  ☐ 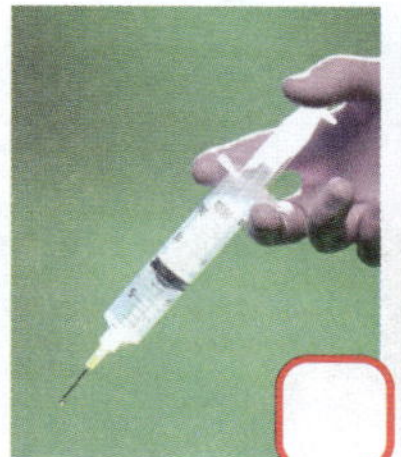 ☐ 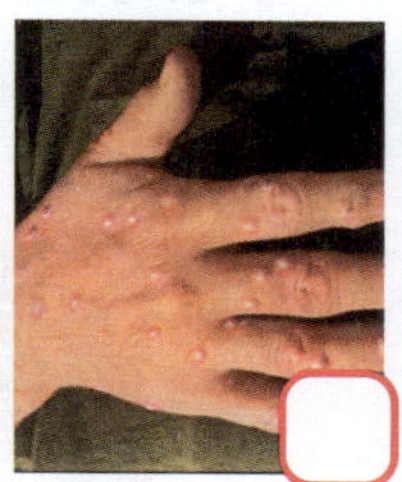 ☐ 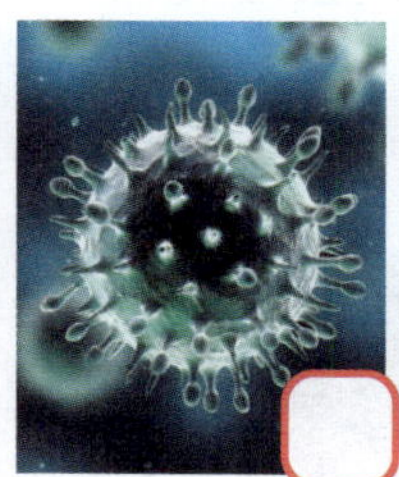 ☐ 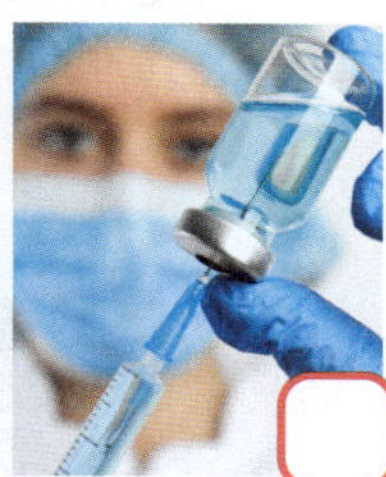 ☐

C Circle the correct option.

Roy: Do you know about an old disease called [1] **smallpox / vaccine / needle** ?

Gustavo: No, I don't. Is it a [2] **cough / vaccine / virus** ?

Roy: Yes, it was.

Gustavo: Is it gone?

Roy: Yes! We don't have it anymore because a scientist discovered a [3] **needle / vaccine / cough** .

Gustavo: That's good!

A Unscramble the words and complete the chart.

Cnehise   Egitypan   Itlaain   Jasneape   Sdisweh   Truskih

-ese	-ian	-ish
Chinese		

B Look and write.

1 He's from Lebanon.

He's _______________ .

2 She's from Italy.

She's _______________ .

3 He's from Türkiye.

He's _______________ .

4 She's from Japan.

She's _______________ .

5 He's from Great Britain.

He's _______________ .

6 She's from Australia.

She's _______________ .

C Choose three countries. Find out their suffixes. Write the countries and their adjectives in your notebook.

A **Complete the paragraphs.**

> liter   cup   hydroponic   sprouted   pests   oxygen

This is my **1** _____________ gardening project. I am using this
2 _____________ to measure a **3** _____________ of water. There
is no soil, so there aren't any **4** _____________ to eat the leaves.
The plants just need light, water, and **5** _____________ to grow.
Look! There are some **6** _____________ seeds over here.

> octopus   marine park   nets   fishing   octopus

We're visiting a **7** _____________ this weekend. On Saturday, we're going to go
8 _____________ . We'll bring our fishing poles and **9** _____________ . Then on Sunday,
we're going diving. I hope we see an **10** _____________ !

B **Complete the dialogues. Use the simple past or the past continuous form
of the verbs in parentheses.**

1 A: **1** _____________________ (you / wait) at the bus stop when
      2 _____________________ (the bus / arrive)?

   B: Yes, I **3** _____________________ .

2 A: What **4** _____________________ (Jenna's sister / do) when
      5 _____________________ (you / visit) her?

   B: She **6** _____________________ (research) hydroponics.

3 A: What movie **7** _____________________ (Jacob / watch) when
      8 _____________________ (his friend / call)?

   B: He **9** _____________________ *The Blue Octopus*. (watch)

Unit 6 and Me

How hard I worked ☆☆☆☆☆   Did I reach my goal? ☺ ☺ ☹

One thing I learned is ____ .

My goal for Unit 7 is ____ .

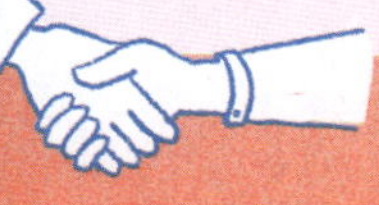

7 What effects can our choices have?

Vocabulary 1

A Match the sentences to the pictures.

1 She didn't say hello to anyone. Is she arrogant?

2 Woah! I can't see him. He's invisible.

3 They aren't saying nice things about her. They're being mean.

4 She isn't afraid to climb the wall. She has courage.

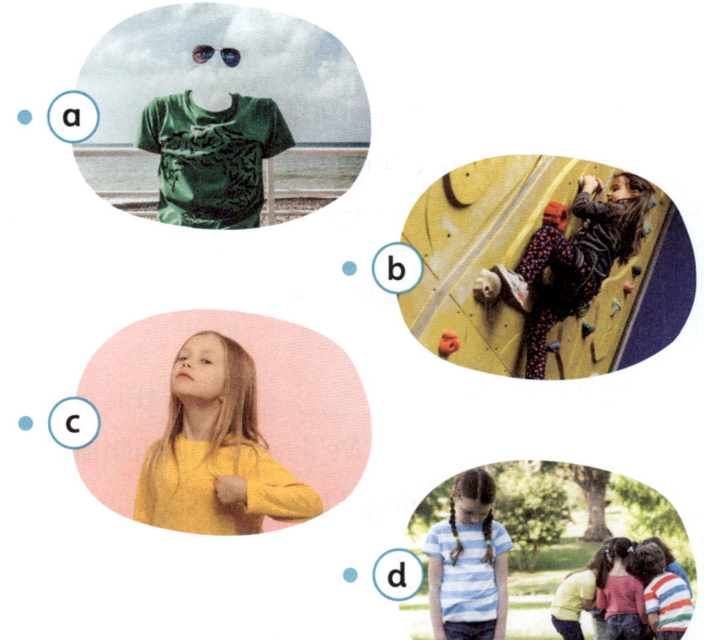

a

b

c

d

B Complete the texts.

argue   ignored   negative

My best friend didn't talk to me at all yesterday.
She ¹ _______________ me! This made me feel
² _______________ . I don't want to ³ _______________
with her, but I do want to talk to her about it.

advice   grown-up   positive

When I have a problem, I talk to a ⁴ _______________ like
my dad. He always gives good ⁵ _______________ and
helps me feel ⁶ _______________ about everything.

Who do you talk to when you need advice? Why?

A **Unscramble the sentences.**

1 I / talk / going to / . / to the new student / am

____

2 is / . / Hanna / going to / introduce everyone

____

3 write / . / thank-you notes / We / going to / are

____

4 He's / the whole class / going to / . / invite

____

B **Complete the sentences.**

1 My friends and I _are not going to play_
   (not play) soccer after school today. We
   _______________________________ (play) Frisbee.

2 Today, AJ _______________________________ (eat)
   a sandwich, but he _______________________________
   (not eat) an apple.

3 Lara _______________________________ (not use) her tablet
   before bed tonight.

4 This evening, I _______________________________ (not go)
   to the library. It's my mom's birthday, so we
   _______________________________ (go) to a restaurant.

1 A: _______ Is _______ Rafa <u>going to bake</u> cookies? (bake)

B: _____ Yes, he is _____ .

2 A: _______________ Bindiya _______________ gymnastics? (do)

B: _______________ .

3 A: _______________ they _______________ lunch with the new student? (eat)

B: _______________ .

4 A: _______________ they _______________ cartoons? (watch)

B: _______________ .

D Use the code to write the questions.

1	2	3	4	5	6	7	8	9	10	11	12	13
a	b	c	d	e	f	g	h	i	j	k	l	m

14	15	16	17	18	19	20	21	22	23	24	25	26
n	o	p	q	r	s	t	u	v	w	x	y	z

1 23 8 1 20   1 18 5   25 15 21   7 15 9 14 7   20 15   4 15   1 6 20 5 18   19 3 8 15 15 12?

<u>W h a t</u> _______________________________

2 23 8 1 20   9 19   19 8 5   7 15 9 14 7   20 15   5 1 20   6 15 18   4 9 14 14 5 18?

____

3 23 8 1 20   1 18 5   20 8 5 25   7 15 9 14 7   20 15   20 1 12 11   1 2 15 21 20?

____

Letters to Aunt Noor

Hi, everyone. I'm Aunt Noor! Do you need some advice?
Write to me with your problem. Maybe I can help you!

Hi Aunt Noor,

Yesterday, I won the school spelling bee. I was so excited! I thanked almost everyone, but I forgot to thank my best friend. I didn't plan to ignore her, but she looked very unhappy. Before the spelling bee, she visited my house every night and helped me practice. Last night, she didn't visit. I feel terrible.

Worried Winner

Dear Worried Winner,

You are feeling bad because you forgot to thank your friend. Everyone forgets sometimes. I think you should tell her you're sorry. I'm sure she'll understand you were excited. Maybe you can help her with something soon.

Aunt Noor

Hi Aunt Noor,

I'm at a new school, and I don't have any friends. I sat alone in the cafeteria at lunch today. I felt invisible. At my old school, I had a lot of friends. Every night, I text my friends from my old school. Am I going to be sad and lonely at my new school forever?

Lonely at Lunch

Hello Lonely at Lunch,

It's hard to be new. It's OK to feel lonely at your new school. Try talking to one new person every day. Stay positive and have courage. Be friendly to your classmates. Then they'll be friendly to you, too!

Aunt Noor

B **Underline these words in the text.**

advice   ignore   invisible   positive   courage

C **Who is Aunt Noor's advice for? Write *WW* (Worried Winner) or *LL* (Lonely at Lunch).**

1 Everyone forgets sometimes.   _____

2 Try talking to one new person every day.   _____

3 Maybe you can help her with something soon.   _____

4 I think you should tell her you're sorry.   _____

5 Stay positive and have courage.   _____

6 Be friendly to your classmates.   _____

D **Check (✓) the emotions the writers feel.**

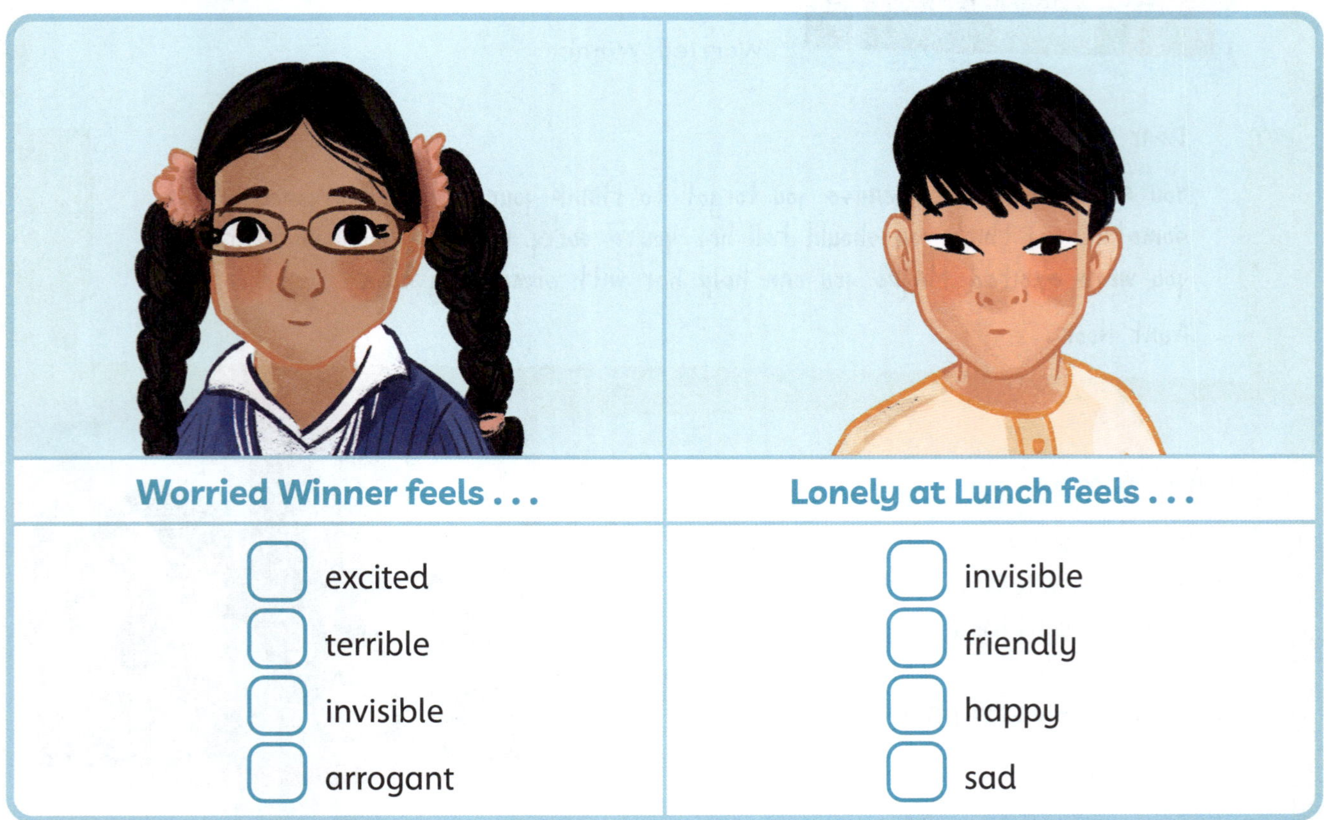

Do you agree with Aunt Noor's advice?
What other advice do you have for the writers?

A **Circle the correct option.**

1 Petra finished playing tennis. She wants to **take a shower** / **donate** / **future** now.

2 Carol, please don't **waste water** / **donate** / **take a shower**. Use it for the plants.

3 They want to **barren** / **future** / **donate** food to help others.

4 We have to take care of the **waste water** / **environment** / **disposable**.

5 This bottle is **barren** / **disposable** / **refillable**. We can use it again and again.

6 We have to throw these bottles away. They are **refillable** / **disposable** / **environment**.

B **Complete the poster.**

> disposable   barren   donate   future   waste water   refillable

We want to help planet Earth, because we want our planet to be healthy. We don't want it to become dry and [1] ______________ .

Tip 1:
Take short showers, so we don't [2] ______________ .

Tip 2:
Don't throw away nice clothes. [3] ______________ them to charity instead.

Tip 3:
Don't use [4] ______________ bottles. Use [5] ______________ bottles to make less trash!

If we do these things, Earth will have a better [6] ______________ .

A Write *True* if the sentence is true. Correct the false sentences.

1 Sometimes my **recorder** runs around in circles. ___________________

2 My **hamster** lives in a bowl of water. ___________________

3 A **classical music** is an easy instrument to learn. ___________________

4 You can **pet** the cat. It's very friendly. ___________________

5 My dad listens to **goldfish** on Saturday mornings. ___________________

6 Where should I go? I can't **decide**. ___________________

B Look at A. Number the pictures to match the corrected sentences.

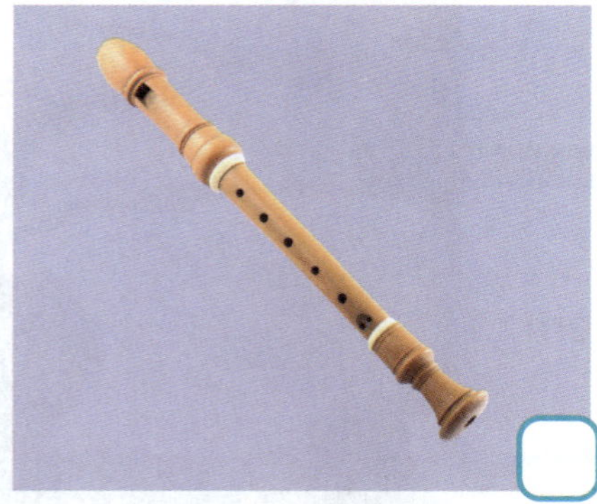  

C Circle the correct options to complete the conversation.

Angelina: Are you going to go to the school's [1] **hamster** / **classical music** / **goldfish** concert on Friday?

Barrak: I'm not sure. What time does it start?

Angelina: At 5:30 pm. They're going to play the songs they learned on [2] **pets** / **goldfish** / **recorders** in music class.

Barrak: I'll [3] **decide** / **pet** / **recorder** this afternoon and tell you tomorrow!

A Read and circle the correct options.

1 We can't decide where to go after lunch. There's
a / an / the ice cream shop and **a / an / the** cake shop
at the mall. **A / An / The** ice cream shop has 43 different
kinds of ice cream, and **a / an / the** cake shop has
yummy chocolate cake. Maybe we don't have to
decide. We can get **a / an / the** ice cream cake!

2 My parents are going to give my sister **a / an / the** hamster or **a / an / the** goldfish
for her birthday. **A / An / The** hamster is black and white and **a / an / the** goldfish
is orange. Which one should we choose?

3 Talia wants **a / an / the** new sweater. The store has **a / an / the** blue sweater and
a / an / the orange one in her size. Her favorite color is blue. She decides to get
a / an / the blue one.

B Complete the text with *a*, *an*, or *the*.

I can't decide what to do this weekend. I can
go to ¹ __________ Cobras' baseball game or
² __________ City Aquarium. Last year, I saw
³ __________ baseball game. It was a lot of fun.
I even caught ⁴ __________ ball! ⁵ __________
baseball game is on Saturday night, but
⁶ __________ aquarium is open all day. We can
see ocean animals and walk around for hours.
There are fish, and there is ⁷ __________ octopus,
too! I think I'll go to ⁸ __________ aquarium.

C Go to your notebook. Write three sentences about your choices for this weekend. Use B to help you.

On the weekend, I can …

A **Two of the three options are correct. Cross out (X) the wrong option.**

1 **Pets:** a hamster   b goldfish   c barren
2 **Negative actions:** a to have courage   b to argue   c to ignore
3 **Ways to describe plastic bottles:** a refillable   b mean   c disposable
4 **Ways to describe emotions:** a negative   b positive   c advice
5 **Negative ways to describe a person:** a arrogant   b mean   c courage
6 **Verbs:** a donate   b argue   c recorder

B **Complete the conversation with *going to* and the verbs in parentheses.**

Patricio: I ¹ _____ am not going to waste water _____
(not waste water) in the bathroom.

Elena: Really? What ² _________________
_________ (do)?

Patricio: First, I ³ _________________
(take) shorter showers. Then I
⁴ _________________ (use)
refillable shampoo bottles.
I ⁵ _________________
(not buy) toilet paper or soap covered
in plastic.

Elena: ⁶ _________________
(turn off) the water when you brush your teeth?

Patricio: Oops! Yes, ⁷ _________________ . Good idea!

Unit 7 and Me

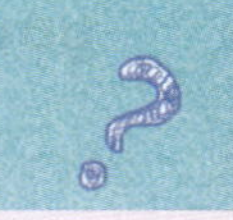

How hard I worked ☆☆☆☆☆   Did I reach my goal? ☺ ☺ ☹

One thing I learned is _________________________________.

My goal for Unit 8 is _________________________________.

8 Who can affect our choices?

Vocabulary 1

A **Circle the correct option.**

1 My science **chapter** / **partner** / **member** and I work together in class.

2 Today, we will do **an experiment** / **a biography** / **a superhero** with our science teacher.

3 Our **character** / **meeting** / **biography** is at 3:30 this afternoon.

4 Listen! The principal is making **a partner** / **a mystery book** / **an announcement**.

B **Complete the texts.**

| biography   chapter   mystery book   members |

The **1** ______________ of the book club are reading the **2** ______________ of a famous American named Ruby Bridges. They are on the last **3** ______________ . Next, they're going to read a **4** ______________ called *The Clue*. It sounds really interesting!

| character   superhero   announcement |

Mitch is going to the library today. He heard an **5** ______________ about Comic Book Week. There are special events happening. Today is Costume Day. Everyone is dressed as their favorite **6** ______________ , like Mr. Invisible or Cobra Girl. Mitch is the main **7** ______________ from his favorite comic book, *Ice Man*!

How do you choose the books you read?

Grammar

A Complete the sentences with _will_ or _won't_.

1 Barry _______________ read an exciting mystery book tonight. He _______________ read a biography.

2 Heba _______________ say hello to Jill. She _______________ ignore her friend.

3 Tina _______________ work alone today. She has a partner, Beyza. They _______________ do an interesting science experiment together.

4 Riku _______________ walk to school today. He _______________ ride his new bike.

B Look at the schedule. Write sentences using _will_ or _won't_.

1 They won't make puppets at 3:30.
(make puppets / 3:30)

2 _______________________________________
(science experiments / 11:00)

3 _______________________________________
(have lunch / 12:30)

4 _______________________________________
(write superhero stories / 9:30)

5 _______________________________________
(do an obstacle course / 3:30)

 Complete the dialogues with *will* or *won't* and the word in parentheses.

1 **A:** ___________________ at the science club meeting at four o'clock? (she / be)

   B: Yes, she ______________ .

2 **A:** ___________________ tennis on Wednesday? (he / play)

   B: No, he ______________ . He has soccer practice.

3 **A:** ___________________ superhero costumes tomorrow? (they / wear)

   B: No, they ______________ .

4 **A:** ___________________ a mystery book for his book report? (he / read)

   B: Yes, he ______________ .

 Unscramble the questions.

1 What / will / ? / after school / Alfonso / do

____

2 Mary / ? / go / will / Where / on Saturday

____

3 Where / on Friday / play tennis / Fatima / ? / will

____

4 Hassan and Oscar / meet / ? / with the chess club / When / will

____

Where will you be at four o'clock tomorrow?

A Read the panel story. When is Club Day?

Club Day

Hernan is a new student. He's in Ms. Wilson's class. He moved to the United States from Guatemala, and he wants to make friends.

1 On Monday…

2 On Thursday…

3 A few minutes later…

4 After that…

B Underline these words in the text.

announcement   experiments   mystery books
meeting   superheroes   members

C Write the correct answer.

1 How many clubs does Hernan join? _______________________

2 What does Grant give Hernan? _______________________

3 What does Hernan forget? _______________________

4 Who helps Hernan choose a club in the end? _______________________

5 Which club is Hernan's favorite? _______________________

D Complete the character map.

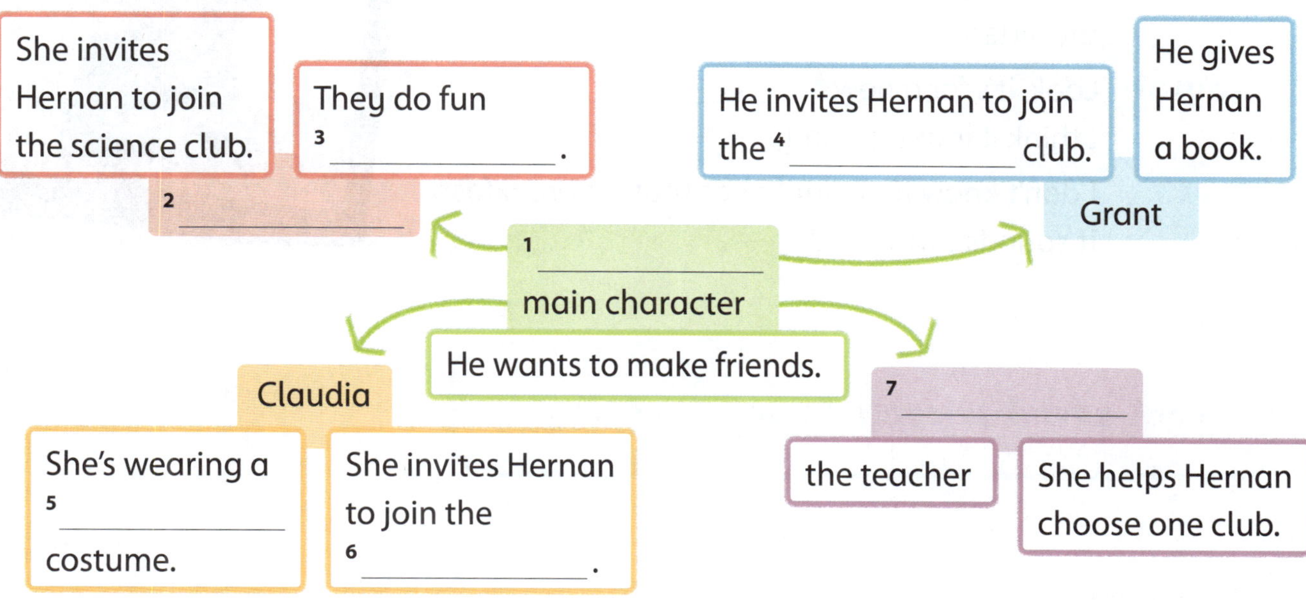

A **Check (✓) the correct option.**

1 I like to pretend. I want to be … when I grow up.

- [ ] an actor
- [ ] a polar bear
- [ ] lemonade

2 My mom likes shopping for clothes and shoes at the … .

- [ ] advertisement
- [ ] department store
- [ ] product

3 This new … comes in three flavors: strawberry, coconut, and chocolate.

- [ ] advertisement
- [ ] polar bear
- [ ] product

4 Would you like some … to drink?

- [ ] department stores
- [ ] experts
- [ ] lemonade

B **Complete the conversation.**

> advertisement   experts   polar bears   breakfast cereal

Taylor: Would you like to watch this video about
1 __________________ in the Arctic with me?
We can learn about how they live from
2 __________________ in science and the
environment.

Briana: Sure! Oh, no! We have to watch an
3 __________________ before we can watch
the video.

Taylor: Look, it's for a new **4** __________________ .
I think it looks yummy.

Briana: I don't know if I want to eat that for breakfast.
It sounds too sweet!

What advertisements do you like? Why?

A Match the sentences to the pictures.

1 My mom is my role model because she works hard.

2 I admire my mom. She's really good at lots of things.

3 This scientist studies vaccines.

4 A vet helps cats, dogs, and other animals.

5 Bea can run fast. She's a really good athlete.

6 We saw a crocodile at the zoo.

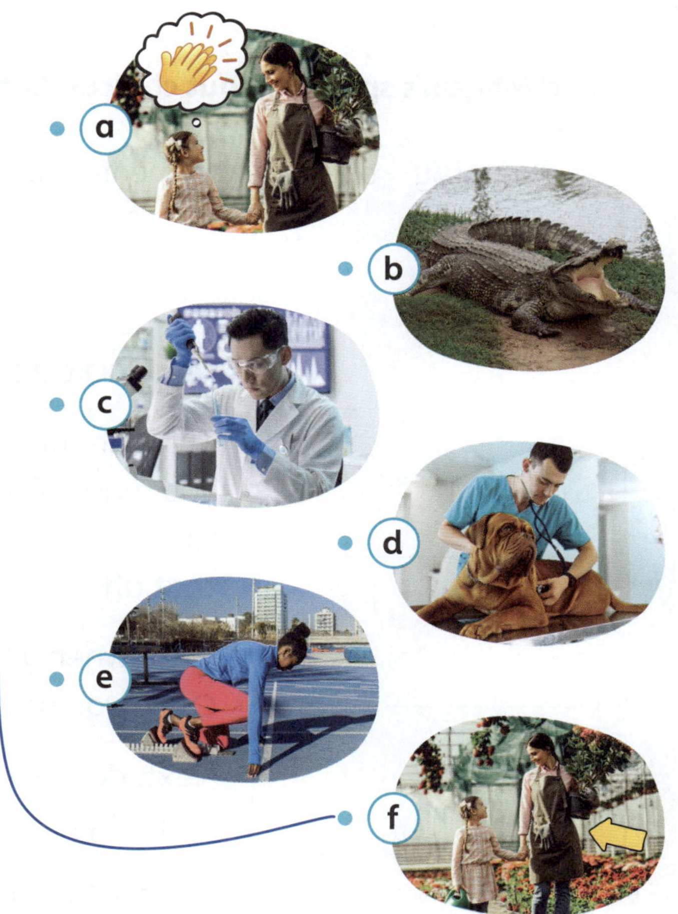

B Complete the texts.

athlete   scientist   role model

admire   crocodiles   vet

My mom studied chemistry and biology. She works as a ¹ _____________ . In her free time, she swims and goes hiking. She's a really good ² _____________ ! She's my ³ _____________ .

My dad is a doctor, but he doesn't help people. He helps wild animals, like lions, bears, monkeys, and ⁴ _____________ . He is a ⁵ _____________ . I ⁶ _____________ him because he has courage!

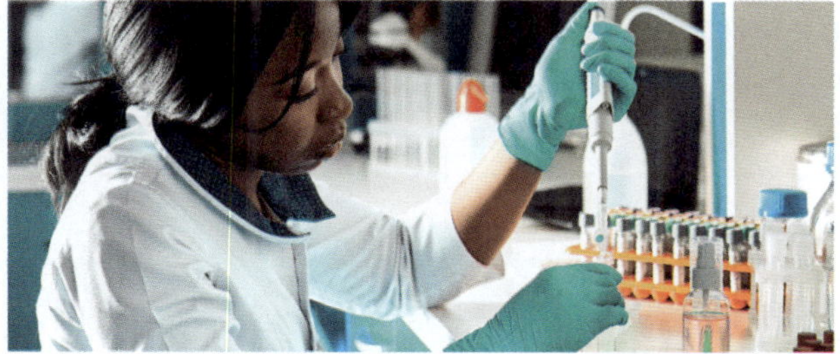

Who do you admire? Why?

A **Read Magda's speech about choices. Label the parts of the speech.**

summary   opening statement   main points

My Choices

1

Think about the choices that you make. Today, I'm going to talk about three kinds of choices that affect your feelings.

2

First, when you wake up in the morning, do you stay quiet? Or do you say "Good morning" to everyone?

Next, do you keep your room tidy? Or do you leave it messy?

Third, who do you spend time with on the weekend? Do you play with your friends or brothers and sisters? Or do you spend all your time alone?

3

These are all choices that affect your feelings. I hope you make choices that make *you* happy. Thank you!

B **Plan your speech about choices. Write your ideas in the chart.**

Opening Statement	
Main Point 1	
Main Point 2	
Main Point 3	
Summary	

C **Go to your notebook and write your own speech.**

D **Check your writing. Use the checkist on page 176 to help you.**

A **Complete the texts.**

1 We did an e _ _ _ _ _ _ i _ _ n _ in science class. We made paper planes in pairs. My _ _ a _ _ n _ _ r ' s plane flew the best. She loves science and wants to be a _ _ c _ _ _ t _ s _ .

2 Felicia is reading an exciting _ _ y _ _ e _ _ _ b _ _ _ _ . The main _ c _ _ a _ _ _ _ t _ _ _ is a girl, just like her! Will they solve the mystery in the last _ _ h _ p _ _ _ r ?

3 Do you think this _ _ _ m _ n _ d _ _ is good? It's a new p _ o _ _ _ _ t . I saw an _ _ d _ _ _ _ t _ _ _ m _ _ t about it with a funny a _ _ o _ .

4 The teacher made an a _ _ n o _ _ _ c _ _ _ _ _ _ _ this morning. A famous Olympic _ _ t _ _ l e _ _ e will visit our class tomorrow. I really _ _ d _ _ i _ _ _ him.

B **Complete the conversation with the correct form of *will*.**

Liyana: Where [1] _________________________ after school? (we / meet)

Miguel: The acting club [2] _________________________ in Mr. Mori's classroom. (members / meet)

Liyana: OK. [3] _________________________ my play script. (I / bring)

Miguel: Great! [4] _________________________ costumes. (I / bring)

Liyana: What character [5] _________________________ (you / be)?

Miguel: [6] _________________________ the brother. (I / be) [7] _________________________ the sister? (you / be)

Liyana: Yes, [8] _________________________ .

Miguel: [9] _________________________ practicing after lunch. (I / start)

Liyana: Me too!

Unit 8 and Me

How hard I worked ☆☆☆☆☆   Did I reach my goal? ☺ ☻ ☹

One thing I learned is ____ .

My goal for Unit 9 is ____ .

9 How can we change our habits?

A Write *True* if the sentence is true. Correct the false sentences.

1 Megan loves eating
~~journals~~ for breakfast.
___pancakes___

2 I **arrive** at school at
8 a.m. every morning.
____

3 Talia writes in her
pancake every night.
____

4 Be careful! You could
trip on the rug.
____

5 Benji put the letters in
the **garage**.
____

6 Franco sets his **bruise** for
6:30 a.m. during the week.
____

B Complete the text.

> bruise   garage   grabbed
> hurried   tripped

Emir woke up late this morning. He was
in a rush! First, he **1** _______________
his lunch from the kitchen. Then,
he **2** _______________ into the
3 _______________ to get his bike.
He **4** _______________ over his
sister's bike and fell down. He got a
5 _______________ on his arm. Ouch!

A Circle the correct options to complete the conversation.

Kate: I ¹**might** / **might not** make pancakes for breakfast tomorrow. Are there enough eggs?

Eline: There are only two. How many eggs do we need?

Kate: That ²**may** / **may not** be enough. I think we need three. We ³**might** / **might not** have to buy more.

Eline: Do you think Mom or Dad ⁴**may** / **may not** go to the supermarket later?

Kate: I don't know. It's late. Let's ask Dad. He ⁵**might** / **might not** know how many eggs we need.

Eline: Dad, how many eggs do we need to make pancakes?

Dad: Two! Are there any strawberries? I ⁶**might** / **might not** make fruit smoothies.

Eline: Sorry, Dad. The strawberries are gone. I ate them!

B Match the sentences.

1 I want to get more sleep tonight.

2 I want to be on time for school tomorrow.

3 I want to eat more fruit.

4 It may rain tomorrow.

a I might ask for another apple or orange.

b I might take an umbrella.

c I might leave the house a little earlier than usual.

d I might go to bed earlier.

may rain   might score   might go   may not go

1 I _______________ a goal during the game on Saturday. That would be great!

2 Look at those clouds! It _______________ this afternoon.

3 On Sunday, we _______________ hiking in the forest as a family.

4 I'm not feeling well, so I _______________ to school tomorrow.

D **Unscramble the sentences.**

1 may play / Eli / . / after dinner / video games

____

2 her bike / . / to school tomorrow / might ride / Jahan

____

3 may not go / to the party / Tanya / . / this weekend

____

4 may not / answer / . / Ruben / the phone

____

5 Dina / for breakfast / might eat / on Saturday / . / pancakes

____

6 in his journal / might not / write / Ha-joon / tonight / .

____

A Read Alana's journal. What does her mom ask her to do?

Alana's Room

March 21

Dear Journal,

Today, Mom was in my room. My things were all over the floor, and she tripped! She got really angry, and I felt bad. She asked me to put some of my old toys in a box. Then, I have to take it to the garage. I have one week! So, I have some work to do!

March 29

Dear Journal,

I put toys and books into a box today. After that, I took everything to the garage. My bedroom is so clean. No one will trip over anything now! Mom and I talked about what to do with the old toys. I might give them to my cousin. Then I remembered my school is having a toy sale next week. So, I might bring them there. I'm not sure what to do yet.

April 2

Dear Journal,

It's four days later, and my room is still clean! Mom is proud of me. We're still thinking about what we may do with my old things. If I bring them to the toy sale, other children can use them. If the school makes money, they can buy things the students need. Those are two good things. I will do that. But my cousin's favorite animal is a rabbit. So, I may give my stuffed bunny to her. That's a good thing, too! :-)

Dear Journal,

Today, I took my toys to the toy sale. Many people arrived early and bought things. One little girl grabbed a teddy bear. She hugged it and smiled. A boy bought some of my comics. He sat down and read one immediately. My old things were new for them. I felt good. The school can buy new sports equipment. My room is really clean. And the best part? My mom is happy!

B Underline these words in the text.

journal   tripped   garage
arrived   grabbed

C Match the causes and effects.

Cause

1 Alana's mom tripped in Alana's room.

2 Alana took her old toys and comics to the garage.

3 Alana brought her old toys and comics to the school toy sale.

4 The school had a toy sale.

5 A boy bought Alana's comics at the sale.

6 A girl bought Alana's teddy bear at the sale.

Effect

a Alana's room was clean.

b She got angry and told Alana to clean up.

c The school got money for new sports equipment.

d Other children bought Alana's old toys and comics.

e She hugged it and smiled.

f He sat down and read one.

D Who makes each choice? Complete the sentences.

Alana   Alana and her mom   a little girl   a boy   the school

1 ___________________________ chooses the old toys to put in a box.

2 ___________________________ choose where to take the old toys.

3 ___________________________ chooses to buy a teddy bear.

4 ___________________________ chooses to buy comic books.

5 ___________________________ chooses how to use the money.

A Circle the correct option.

1 Oops! I made a **clarinet** / **mirror** / **mistake**.

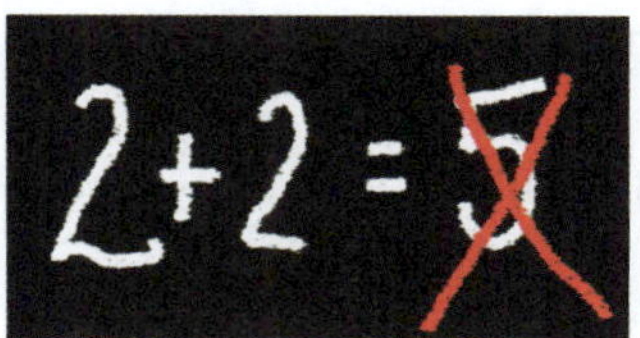

2 Keisha can play the **brain** / **clarinet** / **mirror**.

3 Sam needs to brush his hair, so he's looking in the **fail** / **clarinet** / **mirror**.

4 I use my **brain** / **start** / **succeed** to think.

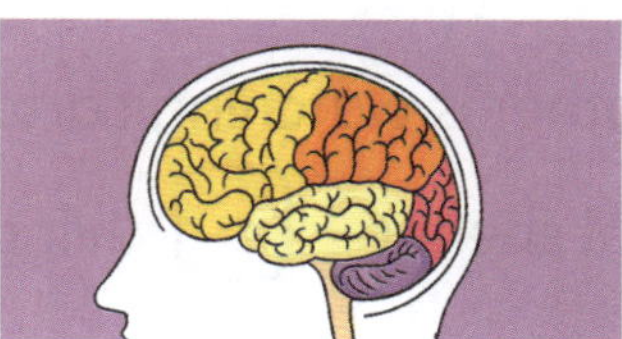

5 My mom uses these bins to stay **mistake** / **organized** / **started**.

B Unscramble the words in parentheses to complete the journal entry.

Dear Journal,

I really want to be more ¹ o_____________ (onizrgaed), but it's hard to ² s_____________ (uesedcc) at this goal. I ³ s_____________ (rttas) the week with everything in its place. I look in the ⁴ m_____________ (rorrim) and say to myself, "This week, you will put things away... right away." But during the week, I ⁵ f_____________ (fila) to do this. What ⁶ m_____________ (kattmesi) am I making?

Lizzie

How do you stay organized?

A Check (✓) the correct option.

1 We watch TV together in the … .
☐ living room   ☐ level   ☐ animal shelter

2 Every Sunday, Julian talks to his grandparents on a … .
☐ living room   ☐ smartphone   ☐ level

3 Wow! Azula is on the sixth … of this game.
☐ tablet   ☐ animal shelter   ☐ level

4 Why is the … black? Is it broken?
☐ screen   ☐ level   ☐ smartphone

5 My little brother is watching cartoons on the … .
☐ animal shelter   ☐ living room   ☐ tablet

6 Emma got her cat from the … .
☐ tablet   ☐ animal shelter   ☐ smartphone

B Complete the text.   smartphone   living room   screen   level

My brother is sitting on the sofa in the [1] ______________ . He is playing a game on Mom's [2] ______________ . He is looking at the [3] ______________ , so he doesn't make a mistake.
He may get to the next [4] ______________ soon. Then it's my turn!

A Circle the correct verb phrase with *get*.

1 Alan **gets up** / **gets over** early every morning.

2 Bisana and Brenda **get along** / **get out** well.

3 Max! **Get around** / **Get out** of my room!

4 My dad wants to **get over** / **get along** this bad cold soon.

5 Carlos **gets up** / **gets around** on his bike.

6 Don't let the cat **get away** / **get over** !

B Complete the questions. One of the verb phrases isn't used.

> get up   get along   get over
> get away   get out   get around

1 Do you _________________ with your classmates?

2 Do you like to _________________ early?

3 How do you _________________ the city?

4 What's a good way to _________________ a cold?

5 When do you _________________ of school today?

C Write answers to the questions in **B** in your notebook. 

A **Two of the three options are correct. Cross out (X) the wrong option.**

1 **Things you can look at:**	**a** mirror	**b** screen	**c** arrive
2 **Things you can do on a test:**	**a** pancake	**b** succeed	**c** fail
3 **Places:**	**a** smartphone	**b** living room	**c** animal shelter
4 **Things you can do:**	**a** hurry	**b** grab	**c** level
5 **Parts of a house:**	**a** garage	**b** mailbox	**c** bruise

B **Complete the sentences with *may*, *might*, *may not*, or *might not*.**

1 Luis _____________ go hiking on the weekend.

2 He _____________ play basketball with his friends.

3 Zi _____________ play video games tonight.

4 She _____________ read a mystery book.

5 Ziyad _____________ have pancakes for breakfast.

6 He _____________ have cereal and fruit for breakfast.

7 Lynn _____________ practice the clarinet.

8 She _____________ play on her tablet.

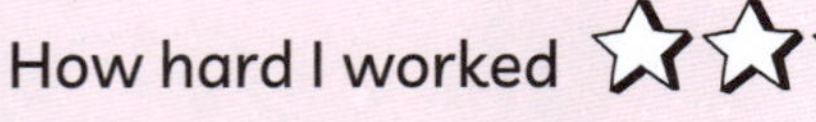

How hard I worked ☆☆☆☆☆   Did I reach my goal?   

One thing I learned is ____ .

My goal for Unit 10 is ____ .

10 Where can we see order in the natural world?

Vocabulary 1

A Complete the sentences with the correct words.

1 This is the r __ __ t __ to the lake.

2 Mr. Owens is l __ __ d __ n __ the children.

3 Look at that __ l __ c __ of birds!

4 That isn't a chicken. It's a g __ __ s __ .

5 The children are c __ __ s __ __ __ g their cars.

6 Are we going in the right d __ __ __ c __ __ __ n?

B Circle the correct option.

Little blue [1] **landmarks** / **penguins** / **goose** live in New Zealand and Australia. They do not [2] **migrate** / **route** / **crash**, but they can travel over 1,000 kilometers when they are a year old. When they are about two years old, they swim to the place they were born. They look for [3] **flocks** / **lead** / **landmarks** along the way to know where to go. When they arrive, one bird leaves the water first and the others [4] **follow** / **migrate** / **flock**. Then, they lay their eggs.

A Circle the correct option.

1 **A lot of** / **A few** birds are in the water.

2 There is only **a lot of** / **a little** water.

3 I can see **lots of** / **a few** birds in the air.

4 **Lots of** / **A few** squirrels are in the grass.

5 There are **a lot of** / **a few** butterflies flying around.

6 I can see **lots of** / **a little** grass in the yard.

B Complete the sentences with *a few*, *a little*, or *lots of*.

1 Can you see _______________ butterflies?

2 I can see _______________ butterflies outside!

3 That lake has _______________ water.

4 This puddle has _______________ water.

5 There are _______________ birds looking for food.

6 There are _______________ birds sleeping.

 Complete the questions with *How much* or *How many*.

1 _________________ birds are near the wildflowers?

2 _________________ wildflowers are in the field?

3 _________________ fruit is in the bowl?

4 _________________ food is on the table?

5 _________________ ants are on the table?

6 _________________ people are at the picnic?

 Look at C. Answer the questions with *a few*, *a little*, or *a lot of*.

1 There are a few bees near the wildflowers.

2 ____

3 ____

4 ____

5 ____

6 ____

How many birds can you see outside?

A **Read the blog. Which animals does Carla write about?**

Animals Moving in North America

Welcome to my blog! This week, I'm writing about how animals use order in different ways. Let's learn more about where, when, and why they move!

Moving Through the Air

Snowy egrets migrate in small flocks. Sometimes, they travel with other birds!

Snowy egrets have white feathers, black beaks, black legs, and bright yellow feet!

Every September and October, a lot of them fly from northern parts of the USA to Mexico, Guatemala, Costa Rica, and other places in Central America for the winter.

Snowy egrets travel in groups, but they don't fly in a V-formation, like Canadian geese. They migrate using the same route every year. It can be 3,000 kilometers long. A lot of egrets go to Lake Chapala in Mexico in the winter.

Moving Through the Water

Every year, about 24,000 gray whales migrate from Alaska, USA to Mexico. It's a very long trip – 5,000 to 7,000 kilometers each way! The whales leave Alaska because it's very cold, and there's little food in winter. They swim to Mexico because it's warm and there's more food there.

Gray whales eat a lot in the summer to have energy for their long winter journey.

When they arrive in the warm water, something special happens. The whales have their babies, called calves. In March, the weather warms up in Alaska, and there is more food again. Then, the calves follow their mothers home. They swim north together, in the direction of Alaska.

Moving on the Land

Mountain lions are also called pumas or cougars. They live in North, Central, and South America, but few people see them. They live alone and hunt at night. Each male has its own hunting area, called a range. If another male arrives, they may fight. Females share their ranges with males and other females. This is one way they keep order, even though they live alone.

Some mountain lions look for food in the snow. They follow animal tracks and movement. Others mountain lions migrate to escape the cold weather in the northern USA and Canada to warm weather in the southern USA and Mexico. That way, they can find more food.

Some mountain lions migrate for food, but others stay and hunt in the snow.

B **Underline these words in the text.**

migrate   flocks   geese   route   follow   direction

C **Answer the questions.**

1 When do snowy egrets migrate?

2 Where do snowy egrets go in the winter?

3 How many kilometers do gray whales migrate?

4 What special thing happens when the whales arrive?

5 Where do mountain lions live?

6 How do mountain lions keep order?

D **Mark the text features in the blog post.**

1 Put a triangle (▲) next to the title.

2 Put a star (★) next to each heading.

3 Put an arrow (➔) next to each caption.

4 Put a dot (•) next to each photo.

A **Check (✓) the correct options to complete the sentences.**

1 An … studies the stars and planets.

☐ axis ☐ orbit ☐ astronomer

2 The moon moves in … around the Earth.

☐ a galaxy ☐ an orbit ☐ a spin

3 There are a lot of stars in our ….

☐ galaxy ☐ plane ☐ axis

1,000,000

4 A … is a really big number!

☐ size ☐ spin ☐ million

B **Look at the picture. Complete the sentences.**

axis   plane   size   spin

1 The planets in our solar system orbit the sun on the same ______________ , like a flat pancake in space.

2 As the planets orbit, they ______________ . Different planets turn at different speeds.

3 The Earth takes one day to spin on its ______________ , but Mercury takes 59 days.

4 Do you know the ______________ of Mars? Is it bigger or smaller than the Earth?

Would you like to be an astronomer? Why? / Why not?

A Match the sentences with the pictures.

1 A hexagon is a shape with six sides.

2 Look at that big tree stump!

3 A beekeeper must wear special clothes.

4 A honeycomb has a lot of holes.

5 Poppies are my favorite flower.

6 The four sides of a square are the same length.

B Check (✓) the correct option.

1 This shape has six sides.
- ☐ length
- ☐ honeycomb
- ☐ hexagon

2 This person collects honey.
- ☐ beekeeper
- ☐ poppy
- ☐ honeycomb

3 You could sit on this part of a tree.
- ☐ beekeeper
- ☐ stump
- ☐ length

4 This flower is red.
- ☐ honeycomb
- ☐ poppy
- ☐ stump

5 You can find a lot of bees here.
- ☐ hexagon
- ☐ beekeeper
- ☐ honeycomb

6 You can measure to find this.
- ☐ length
- ☐ poppy
- ☐ stump

A **Rewrite the sentences with correct capitalization.**

1   If you go to lebanon, visit the National Museum of beirut.

____

2   There is an amazing shopping mall in dubai in the united arab emirates.

____

3   hawaii, new york, and texas are three states in the usa.

____

4   Iguazu Falls is in south america. It's in argentina, but it is very close to paraguay
and brazil.

____

5   The city with the most people in europe is istanbul, which is in türkiye.

____

B **Circle the cities, countries, and continents that should be capitalized.**

C **In your notebook, rewrite the text in B with correct capitalization.** 

A Circle the correct option.

1 Birds travel in a group called this.

  a length   **b** stump   **c** flock

2 These birds fly in a V-shape.

  a penguins   **b** geese   **c** landmarks

3 North, South, East, and West are four of these.

  a landmarks   **b** sizes   **c** directions

4 In math class, you might learn about this.

  a plane   **b** orbit   **c** galaxy

5 The Earth does this once a day.

  a spins   **b** follows   **c** migrates

6 This is a shape with six sides.

  a size   **b** lead   **c** hexagon

B Complete the sentences with *a few*, *a little*, *a lot of*, or *lots of*.

1 Jupiter and Saturn have _________________ moons. There are 163 in total!

2 Mercury doesn't have any moons, but Mars has _______________.

3 There is only _______________ water on Mars. There isn't enough to drink.

4 Only _______________ astronauts can go to the moon at a time, just three or four.

5 We saw _______________ stars on our night hike. It was beautiful!

6 Flying to space is really expensive. It costs _______________ money.

Unit 10 and Me

How hard I worked ☆☆☆☆☆   Did I reach my goal?    

One thing I learned is ____.

My goal for Unit 11 is ____.

11 Why do we need order?

A Circle the correct option.

1 Our classroom has a lot of computer **dreams** / **equipment** / **hallways**.

2 Please write the answer on the **shelf** / **marker** / **whiteboard**.

3 Last night, I had a strange **messy** / **dream** / **column**.

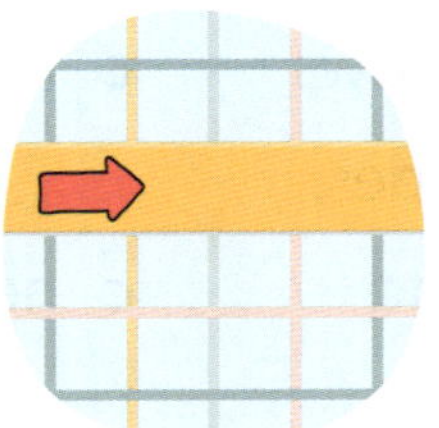

4 **Rows** / **Columns** / **Enters** go from left to right.

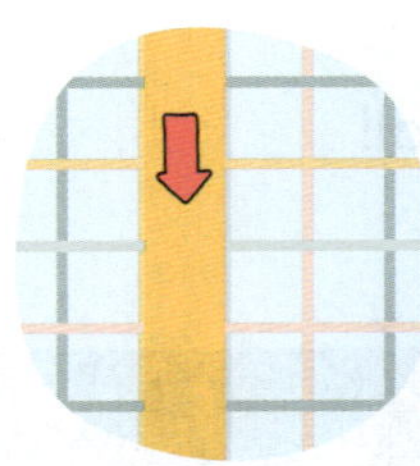

5 **Dreams** / **Equipment** / **Columns** go up and down.

6 That desk is so **messy** / **marker** / **row**!

B Complete the text.

whiteboard   entered   shelf   marker   hallway

In class today, Mr. Garcia asked Grace to write the answer on the **¹** ______________ . Grace said, "I can't find a **²** ______________ ." I pointed and said, "They're over there, on the bottom **³** ______________ ."

Suddenly, we heard a noise in the **⁴** ______________ . The principal knocked on the door and **⁵** ______________ our classroom. She said, "It's time for the pizza party!" We all cheered.

A Complete the chart with the correct form of the adjectives.

Adjective	Comparative	Superlative
big	1	the biggest
small	smaller	2
3	4	the heaviest
light	lighter	5
6	more interesting	7
organized	8	9
10	more colorful	the most colorful

B Circle the correct option.

1 Dalia's shelf is **the highest** / **higher** than Leila's shelf.

2 Noor's shelf is **the messiest** / **messier** than Dalia's shelf.

3 Whose shelf is **more organized** / **the most organized** of all?

4 Which jacket is **more colorful** / **the most colorful**, Dalia's or Leila's?

5 Whose jacket is **more colorful** / **the most colorful** of all?

6 Noor's jacket is **the most colorful** / **more colorful** of all.

1 Corey's backpack is _________________________ Rustam's. (light)

2 Zander's backpack is _________________________ . (heavy)

3 Corey's backpack is _________________________ . (colorful)

4 Zander's backpack is _________________________ one. (small)

D Complete the questions with the comparative or superlative form of the adjectives. Then write the answers in your notebook.

1 Which hamster is _________________________ of all? (small)

2 Which hamster is _________________________ , Bubbles or Miss Patty? (messy)

3 Which hamster has _________________________ clothes, Miss Patty or Cupcake? (colorful)

4 Which hamster is _________________________ of all? (hungry)

E Look at the picture in **D**. Write *yes* / *no* questions and answers in your notebook. 

A: Is Cupcake the biggest hamster?

B: Yes, he is.

A **Read the story. Why is Lucas surprised?**

Lucas and the Library

Lucas loved to read. He wanted to read one book every day. So he went to the library *every day*. He was friends with the librarian, Ms. Lopez, and he always said hello to Nala the library cat, who liked to sleep on the shelf.

"What are you reading today, Lucas?" Ms. Lopez asked.

"A biography about a famous singer," said Lucas with a smile.

"How is it?" said Ms. Lopez.

"It's the most interesting one yet!" Lucas replied.

The next day, Lucas walked into the library. "Hi, Ms.—" Lucas stopped. Things were very different. There weren't any books on the shelves! Some children were watching a movie on an enormous TV! Other children were using markers to draw on the whiteboard.

Nala, the library cat, was wearing glasses and using the computer equipment. Ms. Lopez was helping her.

Lucas asked Ms. Lopez, "Where are all the books?"

Ms. Lopez looked up and said, "In the hallway." Lucas looked in the hallway, but it was too full of books to enter! Oh, no! This was terrible. The library was noisy and messy … and worst of all, he couldn't find any books to read!

Suddenly, Lucas woke up. It was a dream! It was Saturday morning, and he was in his bed. He jumped out of bed and ate his breakfast.

"Can you take me to the library?" he asked his mom.

"Sure, after we have breakfast," she said. "Is everything OK?"

"I don't know. I need to check."

Lucas and his mom arrived at the library. Lucas ran up the stairs and quickly entered. It was quieter and calmer than he remembered.

"Phew!" said Lucas, looking around. "It really was a dream!" He laughed. Then, he walked over to the shelves to pick his book for the day.

B **Underline these words in the text.**

shelves   markers   whiteboard
equipment   dream   entered

C **Read the sentences. Write *dream* or *real*.**

1 Ms. Lopez works at the library.

2 Lucas tries to read a book every day.

3 Nala uses the computer equipment.

4 The books are all in the hallway.

5 Some children watch a movie.

6 Nala sleeps on a shelf.

D **Check (✓) the conclusions you agree with.**

1 Lucas really likes books and reading.

2 Ms. Lopez is an English teacher.

3 Nala the library cat likes computers.

4 Lucas is worried because of his dream.

5 The library is a messy, noisy place.

6 Lucas is happy at the end of the story.

A **Unscramble the words in parentheses to complete the sentences.**

1 This f______________ (ssfilo) is very, very old.

2 I like to sleep on a soft p______________ (lopilw).

3 The beans are in a______________ (ielas) 7.

4 The cars stop when the t______________ l______________ (ficftar ghitl) is red.

5 That r______________ (ugr) has a beautiful pattern!

6 Please a______________ (rgarane) the fruit carefully.

B **Number the pictures to match the sentences in A.**

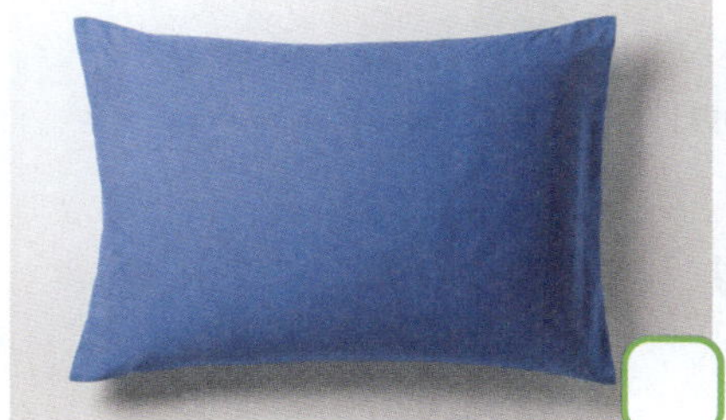

C **Complete the dialogues.**

aisle   crosswalk   traffic light   groceries

1 A: Mom, can we cross the street now?

B: No, let's wait until that ______________ turns green. Then we can use the ______________.

2 A: Hi! Did you find all the ______________ you need?

B: No, I couldn't find the breakfast cereal.

A: Oh, it's in ______________ 9.

A Complete the sentences.

> add   score   divide   multiply   measure   subtract

1 If you ______________ **8** and **12**, you get **20**.

2 If you ______________ **2** from **10**, you get **8**.

3 If you ______________ **9** by **10**, you get **90**.

4 If you ______________ **100** by **20**, you get **5**.

5 Use a ruler to ______________ the paper.

6 Did our team ______________ more points than the other team?

B Complete the conversation.

> add   divide   multiply   subtract

Ayako: How many people are coming to the party?

Mom: Seven. We need to [1] ______________ the cake into ten pieces later.

Ayako: Ten pieces?

Mom: Yes. You, Dad, and I will want cake, so we need to [2] ______________ three pieces for us, too!

Ayako: Oh, right! Do we have enough chairs, Dad?

Dad: Yes, we have twelve chairs. So, we can [3] ______________ two.

Ayako: Oh, no! There are only five sandwiches.

Dad: We need to [4] ______________ that number by two.

Mom: Come on! Let's go in the kitchen and make some more.

What kinds of things do you measure?

A Read the descriptive text. Label its parts.

body   title   introduction   conclusion

1

The Upside Down House

2

Last night, I had the strangest dream! Everything in my house was upside down.

First, I was in my bedroom, but I wasn't walking on the floor. That was below me! When I turned on my light, it lit up from the floor. How strange!

3

I had to walk on the wall to get to my door. When I opened it, the hallway was upside down, too! In the living room, the couch pillows were growing bigger and bigger. They were going to fill the whole room. So, I ran to the kitchen. When I got there, bears were making pancakes, but the pancakes wouldn't stay in the pan. What a mess!

4

When I woke up, everything was normal. I was happy that everything was the right way up again!

B Plan to write a descriptive text.

My Dream

Event 1

Event 2

Event 3

C Use your plan in **B** to write a descriptive text in your notebook.

D Check your writing. Use the checklist on page 176 to help you.

A Two of the three options are correct. Cross out (X) the wrong option.

1 **Things in a bedroom:**   a   a rug   b   a pillow   c   groceries

2 **Things you do in math class:**   a   add   b   column   c   subtract

3 **Things in a science classroom:**   a   a dream   b   a fossil   c   equipment

4 **Actions you do:**   a   score   b   measure   c   hallway

5 **Things in the street:**   a   traffic light   b   crosswalk   c   pillow

6 **Things in a grocery store:**   a   aisles   b   fossils   c   shelves

B Complete the sentences with the comparative or superlative form of the adjective in parentheses.

1 A whale shark is _________________ shark in the ocean. (big)

2 A zebra is _________________ than an elephant. (small)

3 The cheetah is _________________ land animal in the world. (fast)

4 A hippopotamus is _________________ a dog. (heavy)

5 The hummingbird is _________________ bird in the world. (light)

6 A toucan is _________________ a sparrow. (colorful)

7 What is _________________ animal in the world to you? (interesting)

Unit 11 and Me

How hard I worked ☆☆☆☆☆   Did I reach my goal?    

One thing I learned is ____.

My goal for Unit 12 is ____.

Vocabulary 1

A Complete the chart.

~~adjectives~~   images   nouns   rhyming words   syllables   verbs

1 adjectives	2	3
tall sweet beautiful	drink talk write	cat–mat think–drink name–game

4	5	6
per • son ba • na • na con • ver • sa • tion		a dream a car a house

B Circle the correct option.

1 **A:** What do you see through the window?

   B: I **adjective** / **observe** / **syllable** the children playing.

2 **A:** How do I write a poem?

   B: It's really easy! Just follow the **instructions** / **verbs** / **sentences** .

3 **A:** What is an example of a complete **image** / **sentence** / **instruction** ?

   B: I am a student.

4 **A:** Does your dad write stories?

   B: No, but he writes poems. He's **a noun** / **a poet** / **an image** .

Point to an image you like. Why do you like it?

A **Read and circle *True* or *False*.**

1 This kite is as colorful as that one.

True   **False**

2 This turtle is as happy as that one.

True   **False**

3 This frog is as small as that one.

True   **False**

4 This flower is as short as that one.

True   **False**

B **Unscramble the sentences.**

1 I'm / as / . / as / my brother / fast

____

2 colorful / as / mine / . / Their pictures / as / are

____

3 tall / . / as / as /my mom / I'm / not

____

4 as / long / . / mine / Carla's poem / as / isn't

____

5 Kimi / aren't / organized / My friends and I / . / as / as

____

C **Complete the sentences with the comparative adjective and *as*.**

1 Puebla isn't ______ *as sunny as* ______ Cairo today. (sunny)

2 Cairo isn't ________________________ Puebla today. (rainy)

3 The leaves in Brasília aren't ________________________ the leaves in Seoul. (colorful)

4 The leaves in Seoul aren't ________________________ the leaves in Brasília. (green)

D **Read the poems. Then answer the question.**

Poem A

Flutter, flutter
Butterflies land on flowers.
Tweet, tweet
Birds sit on branches.
Whoosh!
The wind moves the clouds.
Spring is here again.

Poem B

1 Is Poem A as colorful as Poem B? ________________________

2 Is Poem A as short as Poem B? ________________________

3 Are the words in Poem A as easy as the words in Poem B? ________________________

4 Are the letters in Poem A as big as the letters in Poem B? ________________________

A Read the information and the poems. How do the poems make you feel?

Let's Write More Poems!

Poets use words to make you see, hear, and feel the images they write about. Most poems use lots of adjectives and adverbs. Here are two more poems to read. Try writing them, too!

I'm Zaina from Lebanon. I like to write funny poems. That's why I like limericks. The instructions are easy.

Limericks

Limericks are usually funny. The first line often introduces a person and a place. They follow an AABBA rhyming pattern, so there are rhyming words at the end of the first two lines. The third and fourth lines rhyme with each other, but the fifth line rhymes with the first two lines.

The Rocket Ship

My friend wanted to go to the moon
We all told her it was much too soon.
  She said, "I'll find a way.
  I'll get there someday."
Good thing we had those balloons!

I'm Felipe from the Dominican Republic. I like telling stories and writing poems. Narrative poems are my favorite because I can mix the two.

Narrative Poems

Narrative poems tell a story and are fun to read out loud. They are like stories, so they can have characters, settings, problems, and solutions. They often rhyme, but they don't have to.

Home Run

Playing baseball in the sun
Pedro's team hasn't won.
It's his turn to hit,
So there's no time to sit.
It's just Pedro and the baseball.

He holds the bat tight.
Will he hit it? He might!
He waits at the plate for the ball.
Here it comes! He stands tall.
It's just Pedro and the baseball.

The ball's as fast as fire.
He wants to hit it higher.
At last, he swings the bat.
Three misses, and that's that.
Today, it wasn't Pedro's baseball.

Pedro's as sad as a lost cat,
But he gets his ball and his bat.
Pedro practices day and night,
So he can hit it just right!
It's just Pedro and the baseball.

The game is on Saturday.
Pedro can't wait to play.
His team is waiting, the crowd, too.
Now, he knows what to do.
It's just Pedro and the baseball.

Crack! The bat hits the ball.
That's how to give it your all!
He did it. It's a home run!
He holds his head high in the sun.
And that's why Pedro loves baseball.

B Underline these words in the text.

poets   images   adjectives
instructions   rhyming words

C Circle the correct option.

1 Zaina's poem is a **haiku** / **narrative poem** / **limerick** .

2 The theme of Zaina's poem is **going to the moon** / **talking to friends** / **buying balloons** .

3 Felipe's poem is **a narrative poem** / **a limerick** / **an acrostic poem** .

4 The theme of Felipe's poem is learning about **fire** / **losing a cat** / **playing baseball** .

D Complete the chart.

Poet	Number of lines	Uses rhyming words	Uses AABBA rhyming	Is funny	Tells a story
Zaina					
Felipe					

A Complete the sentences.

> sequence   mind map   Venn diagram   timeline

1 Use a _________________ to show how things are similar and different.

2 Use a _________________ to help you think of ideas and how they are connected.

3 Use a _________________ to show when things happened.

4 This can also help you put events into a _________________ .

B Number the pictures to match the sentences in **A**.

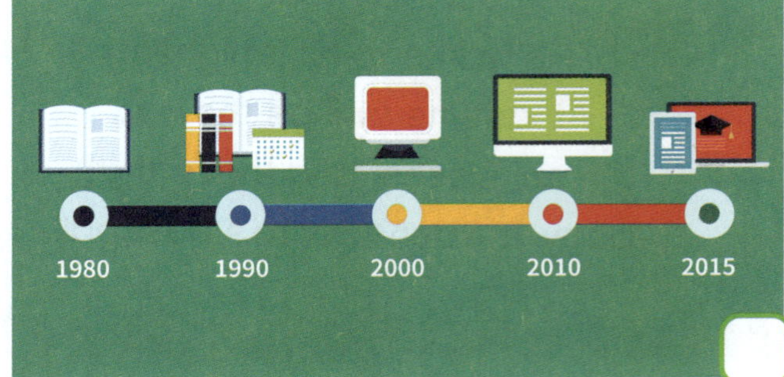

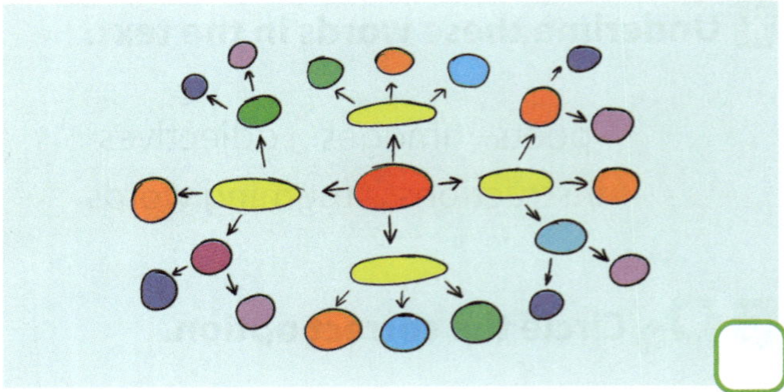

C Unscramble the words in parentheses to complete the conversation.

Rani: Can you help me ¹ b_____________ (stboraminr) some ideas for my story?

Dexter: Sure! What's your story about?

Rani: Well, it's an ² a_____________ (vatrednu) story, and the main character travels around the world looking for a golden tiger.

Dexter: That sounds cool! What are the ³ e_____________ (nevtse) that happen before and after the tiger gets lost?

Rani: I'm not sure. That's what I'm working on now.

Vocabulary 3

A Circle the correct option.

1 Can you remember the **notes** / **lyrics** / **chords** to this song? I forget the words!

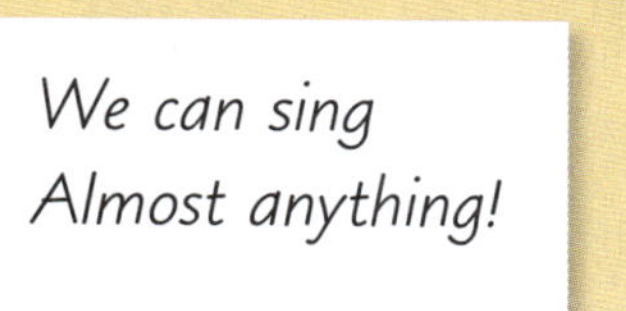

2 Everyone can sing the **chorus** / **chords** / **notes** in this song. There are only two lines, and they're easy!

3 To play a **verse** / **chord** / **lyrics** on the guitar, you have to hold down three different strings.

4 What are you singing? It has a very nice **melody** / **note** / **verse**.

5 Can you read sheet music? How do these **verses** / **lyrics** / **notes** sound?

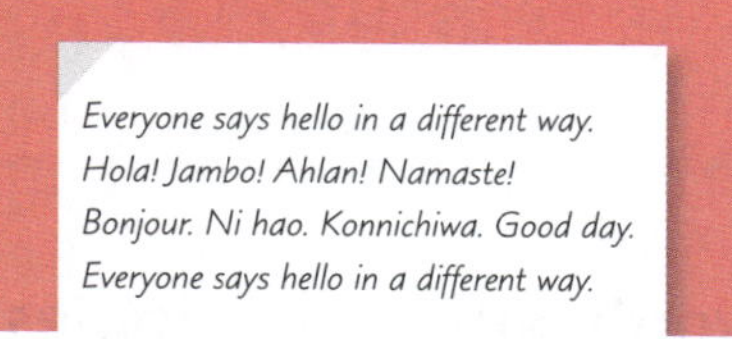

6 This song has three **notes** / **verses** / **melodies**. This is one of them.

B Use the words in A to complete the sentences.

1 I get out my guitar and play a lot of different c______________.

2 When I find a m______________ I like, I feel really happy!

3 I write all the n______________ on sheet music so I remember them.

4 Then, I think of interesting l______________ to go with the music.

5 I decide how many v______________ the song will have.

6 I try to write a short c______________ with just a few lines. That way, more people will sing along!

Can you sing the chorus of your favorite song?

A Draw lines between the syllables.

1 pho|to|gra|pher
2 crocodile
3 pencil
4 computer
5 poet
6 Nigeria
7 gymnasium
8 teacher
9 bicycle

B Write the words from A in the chart.

Two-syllable words	Three-syllable words	Four-syllable words

C Underline the words with two syllables. Double underline the words with three syllables. Circle the words with four syllables.

Joe lives in California. He is in a band. He plays the guitar. He is working on a new song. He has a melody, but not the lyrics. He wants a chorus that is easy to remember. There is a contest at school, and the songs must be done in January.

D Choose four words from this unit and write them below. Draw lines between the syllables.

___________________   ___________________

___________________   ___________________

A **Three of the four options are correct. Cross out (X) the wrong option.**

1 **Types of words:**   **a** noun   **b** timeline   **c** adjective   **d** verb

2 **Parts of a song:**   **a** verse   **b** lyrics   **c** chorus   **d** brainstorm

3 **Ways to organize ideas:**   **a** mind map   **b** timeline   **c** syllable   **d** Venn diagram

4 **More parts of a song:**   **a** adventure   **b** chords   **c** notes   **d** melody

B **Complete the conversation.**

> syllables   connect   poet   rhyming word   lyrics

A: How do you remember the ¹ ______________ in a song? There are so many words!

B: I try to ² ______________ words that go together.

A: How many ³ ______________ are in the word *hippopotamus*?

B: Let's see … Hip-po-pot-a-mus. That's five. Why?

A: Can you think of a ⁴ ______________ for hippopotamus? I'm writing a poem, too.

B: I didn't know you were a ⁵ ______________ ! How about *bus* or *plus*?

C **Rewrite the sentences with (*not*) as + adjective + as.**

1 The sun is bigger than the moon.
The moon ______________________________.

2 The apples and the tomatoes are both red.
The apples ______________________________.

3 An hour isn't longer than sixty minutes.
Sixty minutes ______________________________.

4 Crocodiles are more dangerous than cats.
Cats ______________________________.

Unit 12 and Me

How hard I worked ☆☆☆☆☆   Did I reach my goal? ☺ ☺ ☹

One thing I learned is ______________________________.

My goal for Unit 13 is ______________________________.

13 How can things with the same function be different?

A Complete the sentences with the correct word.

1 People use ice to build __ g __ __ o s.

2 Kings and queens sometimes live in c __ __ t __ __ s.

3 Let's sit outside in the __ __ u __ __ y __ __ d.

4 It's raining. Quick! Let's find s __ __ __ t __ __ .

5 The building has a smooth, circular __ __ m __ on top.

6 Many horses live in the g __ __ __ s __ __ n __ __ __ .

B Complete the text.

ger   grasslands   portable   shelter   stone   wool

I'm Tuya. My family lives in the ¹______________ of Mongolia.
We live in a small village in a ²______________ , not a house.
It's made of light materials like ³______________ , not heavy
materials like ⁴______________ . We move three times a year, so
our home is ⁵______________ . Wherever we move, it gives us
⁶______________ from the wind and cold. I really love our home!

A Circle *True* or *False*.

1 I live in an apartment.
My best friend does, too.
True **False**

2 Amka lives in an igloo.
Lusa does, too.
True **False**

3 My cousins visited a
castle. We did, too.
True **False**

4 Baatar doesn't live in a
ger. Gerel doesn't either.
True **False**

5 Harold has a wool coat.
Marjorie does, too.
True **False**

B Rewrite the underlined sentences using *so*.

1 Jane is cold. <u>Ana is, too.</u>

<u>So is Ana.</u>

2 Pablo is drawing an igloo. <u>I am, too.</u>

____

3 Eshe can see across the grasslands. <u>Fahari can, too.</u>

____

4 I was in the courtyard for the party. <u>They were, too.</u>

____

5 Miriam was in the shelter during the storm. <u>Her parents were, too.</u>

____

1 A turf house isn't made of ice. A ger isn't **either** / **neither**.

2 Stilt houses aren't made of stone. **Either** / **Neither** are igloos.

3 Gers aren't square. Domes aren't **either** / **neither**.

4 Grasslands aren't inside. **Either** / **Neither** are courtyards.

5 Igloos aren't made of wool. Castles aren't **either** / **neither**.

D Complete the conversation with *too*, *so*, *either*, or *neither*.

Reggie: Hi! I live in this building.

Laurence: Really? [1] ________________ do I. We just moved here from Atlanta.

Reggie: Oh, really? My dad is from Atlanta, [2] ________________ .

Laurence: Cool! What do you like to do? I have a bike, but I don't like riding it in the city.

Reggie: I don't [3] ________________ , but I do like skateboarding.

Laurence: Me [4] ________________ ! Let's go together this weekend.

Reggie: OK, but I don't like the skate park on Gold Street.

Laurence: [5] ________________ do I! Let's go to the one on 5th Street.

A Read the photo essay. How many of these homes are on the water?

HOMES ON WATER AND ON WHEELS

There are different kinds of vacation homes. You could stay in a hotel or rent a house. But did you know some vacation homes are portable? Their most important function is to give shelter. But they are also a new kind of adventure!

In Italy, Greece, Croatia, and the Caribbean, there are sailboats for rent. Sailboats are good for amazing adventures because they can travel from place to place. It's a portable home!

Sailboats provide shelter, but there isn't a lot of space. The kitchen is small, and the bedrooms are, too. However, you can see some amazing things from the water and visit beautiful beaches, as well. Families can learn to sail, swim, go fishing, and go diving. They might even see a whale or an octopus!

Canal boats are one way to vacation in the UK, Denmark, and the Netherlands. They are made of wood and usually painted bright colors. They are long and narrow so they can travel on the narrow rivers and canals. Some people call them narrowboats! They are smaller than houses, and they sometimes have small round windows shaped like domes. The kitchen and bedrooms are small. There are places to stop, but you can usually only stay two to seven days. So, canal boats are often on the move! If you like seeing lots of new things, taking a vacation on a canal boat is a great way to see a new country.

Many families in the United States use recreational vehicles (RVs) to take vacations. An RV is a home on wheels. You can drive the RV to a campsite in a park and wake up in a beautiful place, like the mountains. At the park, there is space for the RV and some outdoor space, too. RVs don't have a lot of room inside, but it's OK to sit at tables and chairs outside. It's a little bit like having your own courtyard. RVs come in different sizes, but they are all portable. With an RV, families can make the journey part of the vacation!

B **Underline these words in the text.**

portable   shelter   domes   courtyard

C **Answer the questions.**

1 Where can you rent a sailboat?

2 What can you do on a sailboat vacation?

3 Where can you rent a canal boat?

4 How long can you stay at canal boat stops?

5 Where can you park an RV?

6 Where can you put a table and chairs at an RV park?

D **Complete the chart. Use the photos to help you.**

	has small spaces	stays on the water	stays in a park	has wheels	has a sail	is portable
sailboat	✓					
canal boat						
RV						

Would you like to live in a portable home? Why? / Why not?

A **Circle the correct option.**

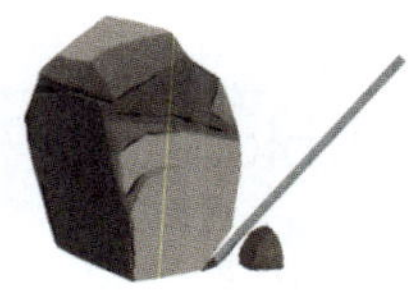 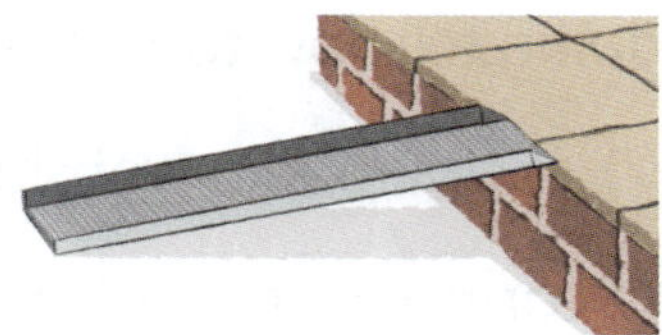 

1 A **lever** / **jar** / **hammer** can help you move things.

2 You can walk up and down this **light bulb** / **ramp** / **force**.

3 You can put small things in a **ramp** / **lever** / **jar**.

 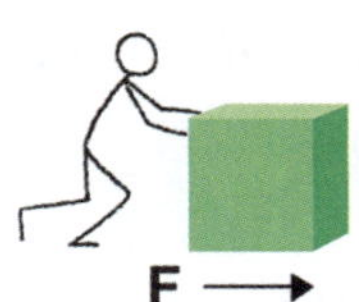

4 Use **scissors** / **ramps** / **screws** to hold pieces of wood together.

5 Use **jars** / **scissors** / **force** to push or pull things.

6 Use a **light bulb** / **hammer** / **jar** to put nails in wood.

7 Use **scissors** / **hammers** / **screws** to cut paper.

8 The room is dark. We need a new **light bulb** / **scissors** / **force**.

B **Complete the text.**   force   lever   ramp

Did you know there are simple machines on the playground? A seesaw is a kind of
¹______________ . Charlie is using ²______________ to push Kate up the ³______________ .

A **Check (✓) the correct option.**

1 Did you hear the … ? It's going to snow tomorrow!

☐ news ☐ social media websites ☐ blog

2 I love watching my favorite cartoons on … after school.

☐ radio ☐ podcast ☐ television

3 My aunt writes about events in her life on a … .

☐ podcast ☐ social media website ☐ television

4 My brother likes to read his favorite soccer player's … .

☐ blog ☐ radio ☐ television

5 My friends and I like to listen to funny … .

☐ radios ☐ podcasts ☐ blogs

6 My mom listens to interviews on the car … .

☐ radio ☐ blog ☐ social media website

B **Number the pictures to match the sentences in A.**

C **Complete the text.**

blog   podcast   radio

I like to listen to music on the [1] ______________ . It's a good way to hear new songs. I also read about the singers on a music [2] ______________ on a website. I listen to a special [3] ______________ , too. It's great because they interview famous singers about their lives.

13 Writing Study

A Complete the chart.

castle   food   hammer   internet   jar
knife   news   newspaper   sugar   weather

Count Nouns	Noncount Nouns
___________	___________
___________	___________
___________	___________
___________	___________
___________	___________

B Complete the sentences with the correct form of the verb in parentheses.

1 Hammers _____________ (fix) many things.

2 The weather _____________ (be) nice today.

3 Yesterday's news _____________ (be) good.

4 This knife _____________ (cut) really well.

5 This blog _____________ (be) so interesting.

C Look at **B**. Underline the subjects of the sentences.

D Use the words in parentheses to write sentences.

1 Castles are made of stone. _____________ (castles / be / made of stone)

2 _____________ (the news / start / 6:00)

3 _____________ (sugar / be / sweet)

4 _____________ (a jar / have / a lid)

E Write three more sentences. Underline the subjects. Circle the verbs.

____

____

____

A **Choose the correct option.**

1 Use **blogs** / **screws** / **force** to hit the tennis ball far.

2 Lions live in the **stone** / **grasslands** / **ramps**.

3 Use a **lightbulb** / **screw** / **hammer** to hit the nail.

4 This building has a **lever** / **blog** / **ramp** for people in wheelchairs.

5 That house is made of wood and **dome** / **stone** / **courtyard**.

6 Outside the castle, there was **a courtyard** / **a television** / **an igloo** with many plants.

7 The lamp won't turn on. We might need a new **screw** / **dome** / **light bulb**.

8 My friends listen to that new **television** / **podcast** / **blog** about movies.

B **Complete the sentences with *too*, *so*, *either*, or *neither*.**

1 **A:** I want to travel around the country in an RV.

   B: I do, _______________.

2 **A:** You can read the news in a newspaper.

   B: You can watch it on television, _______________.

3 **A:** I like listening to science podcasts.

   B: _______________ do I.

4 **A:** I don't use social media websites.

   B: _______________ do I.

5 **A:** I don't know much about cave houses.

   B: I don't _______________.

Unit 13 and Me

How hard I worked ☆☆☆☆☆   Did I reach my goal? ☺ ☺ ☹

One thing I learned is ____.

My goal for Unit 14 is ____.

14 What can have different functions?

A Circle the correct option.

1 You need strong teeth to **bite** / **sneeze** / **dive** into things.

2 We use our fingers and **tongue** / **thumb** / **tears** to hold a pencil.

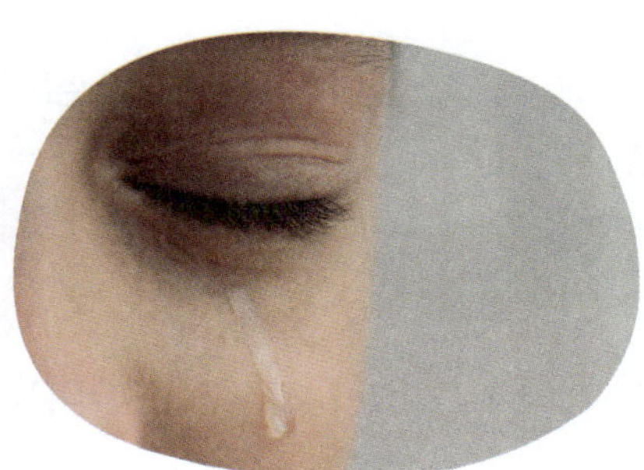

3 There are **cells** / **sneezes** / **tears** on your face. Are you sad?

4 When you learn to swim, you also learn to **lungs** / **float** / **bite**.

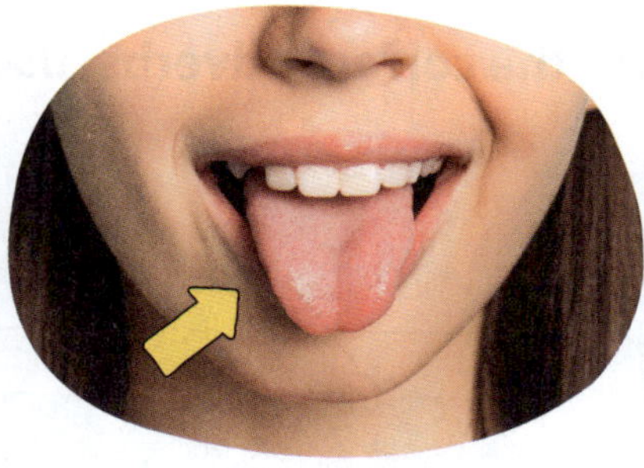

5 We taste food with our **floats** / **ligament** / **tongue**.

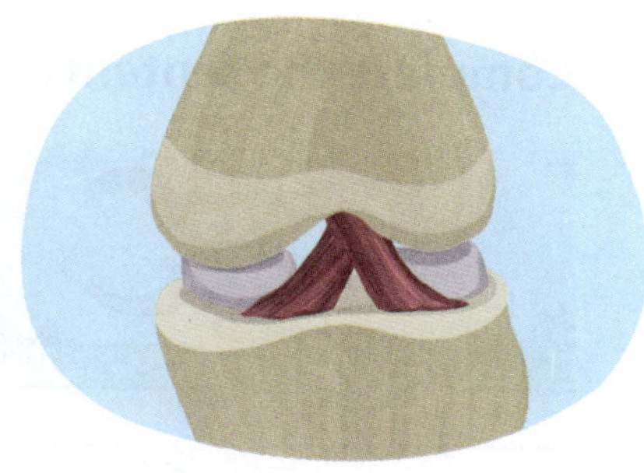

6 **Tears** / **Ligaments** / **Cells** keep our bones together and help us move.

B Unscramble the words in parentheses to complete the text.

I am going to ¹ d_____________ (vedi) into the pool. I take air into my ² l_____________ (lguns). I need air for every ³ c_____________ (clle) in my body. Oh, no! My nose feels strange! I hope I don't ⁴ s_____________ (seznee) while I'm up here. OK. Now I'm ready!

A Complete the chart.

Adjectives		Adverbs	
easy	1		easily
2			beautifully
loud	3		
careful	4		
5			deeply
6			angrily
happy	7		
8			loudly
quick	9		
10			safely

B Complete the sentences with the correct adverbs. Use the chart in **A**.

1 Rosa is a good athlete. She is quick. She runs ____________.

2 I take a deep breath. My lungs help me breathe ____________.

3 Heba likes to be careful. She checks her homework ____________.

4 Don't go too fast when you use that machine. You have to grab the toy ____________.

5 They are happy when they play together. They play ____________.

1 Usain Bolt ran 100 meters in 9.58 seconds.

He / fast / . / ran / so

Wow! _______________________________________

2 Sofia studies her spelling words every day.

very / . / studies / hard / She

____

3 My sister wins many diving contests.

dives / She / well / . / really

____

D Look at **C**. Circle the adverbs.

E Complete the sentences with the correct adverbs.

hard   quickly   slowly   very   quietly

1 Some cells divide fast. They divide _______________,
but others divide _______________.

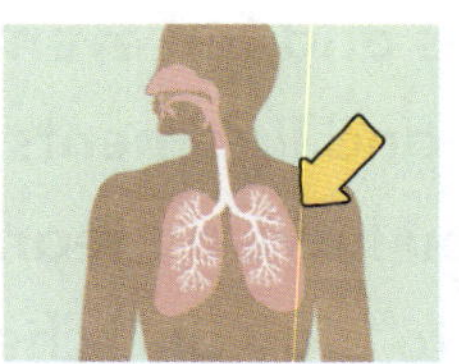

2 Our lungs do a lot of work. They work _______________
all day and night.

3 Tears are _______________ salty.

4 I didn't hear you sneeze. You sneezed so _______________.

What do you do quickly? What do you do slowly?

A **Read the rap poem. What is it about?**

Your Amazing Body

Playing sports helps you stay fit.
You can play a lot or a little bit.
Inside, outside, anywhere,
Your mouth and nose take in air.

Playing sports is good for all,
Tennis, soccer, basketball.
Move and jump, and throw and run,
Make sure to invite everyone.

Eyes and ears, fingers and thumbs,
Take care of them when having fun.
Legs and knees, feet and toes,
Arms, shoulders, and elbows.

For all sports games and fun events
Take care of bones and ligaments,
Warm up well so you have no fear.
Prepare your body to play and cheer.

Water sports are also cool,
Swim and float in the pool.
You can dive from way up high,
Falling quickly through the sky.

Win or lose, short or tall,
Sports are fun for us all.
Score a goal. Do it proudly.
The crowd will cheer very loudly.

thumbs   ligaments   float   dive

C Answer the questions.

1 What helps you stay fit?

2 Which two body parts take in air?

3 What three sports are in the second verse?

4 How can you take care of your bones and ligaments?

5 What can you do in the pool?

6 What will the crowd do if you score a goal?

D ⚙ Check (✓) the best paraphrase of each verse.

Verse 1

☐ a Sports are good for your health, and you can play sports anywhere.

☐ b Sports helps you breathe better, and you can do them a lot.

Verse 2

☐ a Sports are only for some, but basketball and tennis are fun.

☐ b Sports are for everyone, and there are different sports and actions.

Verse 3

☐ a You have to take care of all of your body parts when playing sports.

☐ b Bodies have many parts like elbows, arms, eyes, ears, and thumbs.

Verse 4

☐ a When playing sports, it is important for people to cheer.

☐ b Warm up to get your body ready to play, or you might get hurt.

Verse 5

☐ a You can do sports like swimming and diving in the water.

☐ b Floating in the pool is better than diving through the air.

Verse 6

☐ a Winning isn't the most important thing. It's about having fun.

☐ b Sports are only for those who score goals and win.

A **Complete the sentences with the correct words.**

1 The plant's __ __ __ m is thin, green, and long.

2 The flower's p __ __ __ l __ are a beautiful pink color.

3 Here's an egg. Be careful, so you don't __ r __ __ it!

4 The t __ __ __ t __ __ __ k is very thick and strong.

5 Some animals, like squirrels, __ __ o __ e food for the winter.

6 Trucks help __ __ a __ __ p __ __ t packages from one place to another.

B **Number the pictures to match the sentences in A.**

C **Complete the instructions.**

petals   seedlings   stem   transport

How to Plant a Sunflower

1 First, plant the seeds.

2 Water the soil. This way, the roots can ________________ water to the seeds.

3 After about ten days, the seeds will grow into ________________ .

4 In the next few weeks, the ________________ will grow longer and straighter. Soon, you will see green leaves.

5 After a few months, you will see a lot of pretty yellow ________________ .

A **Complete the sentences.**

crack   gorilla   parrot   scratching   wag

1 What is the easiest way to ________________ nuts?

2 How did that ________________ learn to talk?

3 Why are you ________________ your head?

4 Dogs ________________ their tails when they're happy.

5 This ________________ weighs over 100 kilograms!

B **Circle the correct option to complete the conversation.**

Omar: Did you listen to *The Fascinating World of Animals* podcast?

Beyza: No, I missed it. What was it about?

Omar: It was about animals' amazing bodies. Did you know that cats [1] **wag** / **crack** / **scratch** their tails to communicate? It can mean they're excited, scared, or angry.

Beyza: Oh, that's interesting. Was the podcast all about cats?

Omar: No, they talked about other animals, too. Did you know that an elephant can use its [2] **wag** / **trunk** / **crack** to store water?

Beyza: That's amazing!

Omar: Yeah! And a [3] **parrot's** / **gorilla's** / **trunk's** big toe is like a thumb.

Beyza: Wow! So, it's like they have four hands! I should listen to the podcast.

A Read the essay and label its parts.

different view   ending idea   opinion
reasons   topic sentence   solution

1

2

3

4

5

6

My Laptop by Bruce Williams

I think a laptop is the most useful invention for a student. My laptop helps me in many different ways.

First, it can connect to the internet. I can use it to do research for projects. For example, I can quickly find information about animals.

Next, I can easily type up my projects so they are neat and easy to read.

Finally, I can use it to email my teacher questions. I can also send my homework to her when I'm done.

Some people think it is better to write with a pen and paper.

However, I think that writing on a laptop is better. My laptop helps me stay organized and communicate with my teacher and classmates.

My grandparents didn't have laptops in school. They did research in the library, and they used pens and paper to do their homework. I'm happy that we have laptops now. They're so useful!

B Choose another helpful invention. Then complete the chart.

Invention	Ideas
Why it is useful	
Why some people don't like it	
Conclusion	

C Now go to your notebook and write your own opinion essay. 

D Check your writing. Use the checklist on page 176 to help you.

A **Two of the three options are correct. Cross out (X) the wrong answer.**

		a		b		c	
1	**Human body parts:**	a	tongue	b	thumb	c	stem
2	**Parts of plants:**	a	stem	b	petal	c	attract
3	**Animal actions:**	a	gorilla	b	wag	c	scratch
4	**Action verbs:**	a	drop	b	crack	c	seedling
5	**Things you do with your nose or mouth:**	a	bite	b	thumb	c	sneeze
6	**Things inside your body:**	a	cells	b	lungs	c	trunk
7	**Things you can do in water:**	a	petal	b	float	c	dive

B **Complete the conversation with adverbs.**

A: Doctor, I don't feel [1] _______________ (good).

B: What's the matter. Do you fall asleep [2] _______________ (easy)?

A: Yes, I do. I study [3] _______________ (hard) all day, so I'm tired at night.

B: Are you eating enough food?

A: I think so. But I always feel hungry. And I eat very [4] _______________ (quick).

B: You should try to eat [5] _______________ (slow). Cut up your food [6] _______________ (careful).

A: Anything else?

B: After you eat, sit [7] _______________ (quiet) for a few minutes.

A: Thank you, Doctor. I'll try that.

Unit 14 and Me

How hard I worked ☆☆☆☆☆   Did I reach my goal?   

One thing I learned is ____.

My goal for Unit 15 is ____.

15 How can people improve an object's function?

A Unscramble the words in parentheses to complete the sentences.

1 Some j________________ (tsje) can go faster than 2,400 kilometers per hour.

2 An a________________ (aspihri) is an early kind of plane that looks like a balloon.

3 You can ride in the basket of a h____________ a____________ b____________
(toh ria llobaon).

4 The c____________ m____________ (rwec mmbsere) help everyone on the plane.

5 This p____________ (pgsanesre) likes to sit by the window of the plane.

B Number the pictures to match the sentences in **A**.

C Complete the conversation.

curious   engine   propeller   speed   glider

Emir: Look, I just finished making my toy ¹ ________________ !

Amal: Cool! I'm ² ________________ . How does it fly? Does it
have an ³ ________________ ?

Emir: No, it uses this rubber band. The rubber band turns
the ⁴ ________________ .

Amal: Does it fly fast? What ⁵ ________________ does it go?

Emir: Watch, and I'll show you.

What are you curious about?

A **Underline the adjectives. Circle the prepositions.**

1 Engineers are <u>good</u> (at) math.

2 The astronauts were not happy with the first test flights.

3 Are you interested in propeller planes?

4 I'm curious about how these propellers work.

5 She's excited about the field trip to the flight museum.

6 We were surprised at the airship's history.

B **Complete the conversation with *at*, *with*, *in*, or *about*.**

Mariana: I'm surprised [1] __________ how fast some engines can go.

Benjamin: Me, too! And I'm curious [2] __________ how the wheels go up and down.

Mariana: The museum worker will tell us about that soon. He's very good
[3] __________ explaining things clearly.

Benjamin: What are you interested [4] __________ seeing next?

Mariana: Oh, I really want to see the hot air balloons.

Benjamin: I'm excited [5] __________ riding in one this afternoon.

Mariana: Me, too! I'm really happy [6] __________ this field trip.

C **Underline the adjectives with prepositions in B.**

1 <u>Are they excited about the soccer game?</u> (they / excited / soccer game)

2 ______________________________________ (she / happy / her gift)

3 ______________________________________ (he / surprised / the scary movie)

4 ______________________________________ (they / curious / the experiment)

E **Circle the correct answers to the questions in D.**

1 (Yes, they are.) / No, they aren't.

2 Yes, she is. / No, she isn't.

3 Yes, he is. / No, he isn't.

4 Yes, they are. / No, they aren't.

F **Rewrite the questions in D with *What*.**

1 <u>What are they excited about?</u>

2 ______________________________________

3 ______________________________________

4 ______________________________________

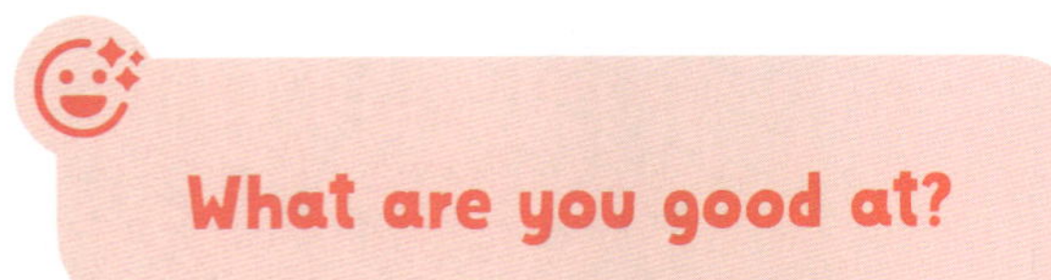

A Read the timeline. How are cars different today than 100 years ago?

Let's Go for a Drive!

Do you travel by car? Do you get excited about going somewhere? Do you wear a seatbelt? Do you look in the rearview mirror? Did you know that seatbelts and mirrors were not part of the first cars? Car makers added things to cars over time for safety. Here is a short history of some of the changes.

1908

Henry Ford makes the "Model T" car in Michigan in the USA. He wants everyone to be able to buy it. He makes them in a new way, so they only cost between $260 and $850. The cars have big, heavy engines. They have no seatbelts.

1921

American Elmer Berger invents the first mirrors in cars so drivers can see the road behind them. The first mirror is on the driver's side of the car. Later, they add one to the passenger side, too.

1959

Swedish engineer Nils Bohlin is curious about car safety. He invents seatbelts for cars. A seatbelt holds the person in the seat if there is an accident. Bohlin wants everyone to drive safely, so he gives the design to all car makers for free.

1971

Italian engineer Mario Palazzetti invents a new kind of brake that stops drivers from crashing. A German car company buys the invention and makes anti-lock braking systems (ABS) cheap and available for many cars.

1998

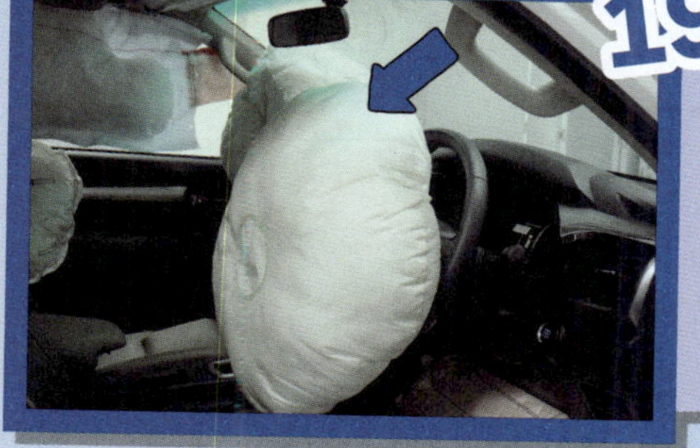

All cars must have airbags now. Airbags are like balloons that fill quickly and keep you safe in an accident. They are inside the steering wheel, in front of the passenger's seat, and in the doors of the cars. They come out if the car hits something.

Today

Electric cars are popular. Some cars can drive or park by themselves, so they don't hit other cars or run over things. These cars can change speed all by themselves.

The Future

Electric cars will get better. People are also doing experiments with solar cars. All cars will be able to drive without drivers, and they will all have the internet!

B Find these words on the timeline in **A**.

engines   passenger   curious   speed

C Write the year for each invention.

1 _______________ airbags

2 _______________ rearview mirrors

3 _______________ Anti-lock Braking System (ABS)

4 _______________ seatbelts

D Put the events in **C** on the timeline.

1908	1921	1959	1971	1998	Today
Model T					electric cars

E Write *True* if the sentence is true. Correct the false sentences.

1 The Model T Ford cost ~~$1,000 to $2,000~~.   _____$260 to $850_____

2 The first car mirror was on the **passenger's** side of the car.   _______________

3 Nils Bohlin designed **airbags** for cars.   _______________

4 Airbags are on the **outside** of cars.   _______________

A **Circle the correct option.**

1 The **rim** / **steer** / **inventor** goes around the inside of the tire.

2 Use the **basketball** / **handle** / **rim** to open the door.

3 If you want to **inventor** / **steer** / **motor** a car, turn the wheel.

4 **Basketballs** / **Handles** / **Trunks** are bigger than baseballs.

5 Can you help me with this box? It's really **handle** / **bulky** / **steer**.

6 Can you help me get the groceries from the **inventor** / **rim** / **trunk** of the car?

B **Complete the conversation.**

Inventors   bulky   motor

Yusuf: Did you hear about the Young [1] _______________ Contest?

Camilla: No, I didn't. What kind of inventions are they looking for?

Yusuf: They want you to take something you use every day and make it function better.

Camilla: So, can you take something big and [2] _______________ and make it smaller?

Yusuf: Yes! Or you can take something that needs a lot of power and make it work better with a [3] _______________ .

Camilla: Sounds great! Let's start brainstorming.

A Correct the underlined words.

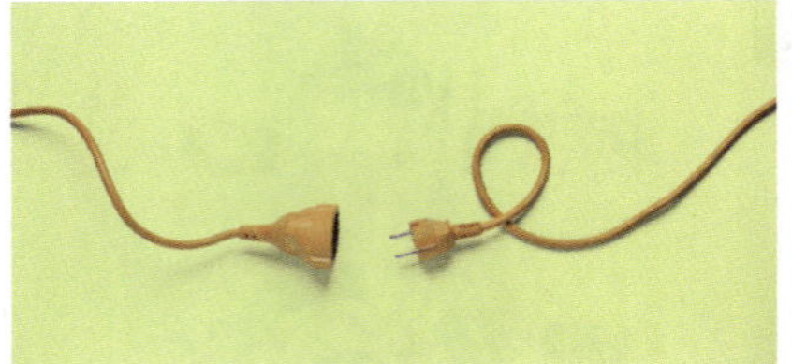

1 Where's the <u>vacuum cleaner</u>? I need it for my computer.

____

2 My grandpa has an old <u>wrist</u>. It still tells time well.

____

3 Caro needs to pack clothes in her <u>cord</u> for her trip.

____

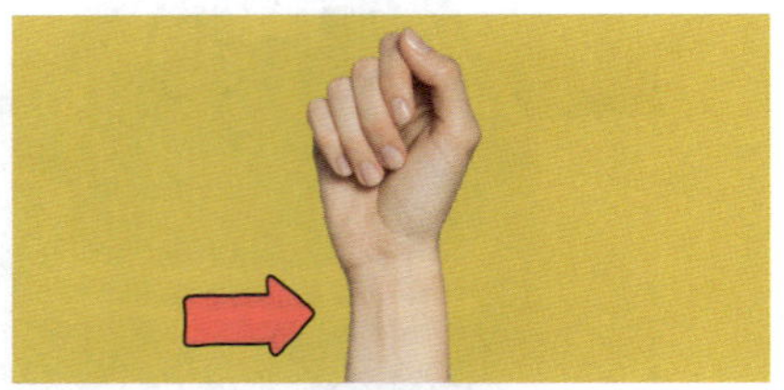

4 After playing tennis for an hour, Aiden's <u>suitcase</u> hurt.

____

5 The blankets are in the <u>pocket watch</u> in the closet.

____

6 There's some dirt on the rug. Where's the <u>trunk</u>?

____

B Complete the conversation.

cord   suitcase   vacuum cleaner   motor

Dad: Look! I bought a new
1 _______________________ .
The **2** _______________________
on the old one doesn't work.

Janine: Finally! Where's the
3 _______________________ ?
I can't see one.

Dad: It doesn't have one.

Janine: Really? It's so small! It looks like it can fit into a
4 _______________________ .

Dad: It might! But it's powerful. Let's give it a try.

A **Circle the correct option.**

1 I don't understand what this extra handle is for. I think it's **useful** / **useless**.

2 The most **useful** / **useless** thing in our classroom is the whiteboard.

3 Our teacher is very **helpful** / **helpless** and kind.

4 I fell in the water, but I couldn't swim. I felt **helpful** / **helpless**.

5 That field of wildflowers is so **colorful** / **colorless**!

6 Water is clear and **colorful** / **colorless**.

B **Complete the text with the correct words from A. Two words are not used.**

Lorena and Fabiola are sisters, but they are very different. Fabiola loves to paint bright pink, purple, and yellow flowers. They are very ¹ _______________. Lorena, however, likes to use pencils to draw pictures of people. Lorena often throws things away. She thinks if something is broken, it is ² _______________. On the other hand, Fabiola fixes things, like the broken vacuum. Thanks to her, it is ³ _______________ again. Lorena and Fabiola are the same in one way. They are both responsible and ⁴ _______________. They help their parents and clean up around the house.

C **Choose three adjectives with *-ful* or *-less*. Write sentences in your notebook.** 

A Circle the correct option.

Reggie: Dad, I'm really excited about our trip to the Grand Canyon!

Dad: Great! So am I. Reggie, please put the [1] **crew member** / **inventor** / **suitcase** in the [2] **pocket watch** / **trunk** / **speed** of the car.

Reggie: OK, done!

Mom: Reggie, did you find your [3] **vacuum cleaner** / **basketball** / **pocket watch**? There's a court near there, and we'll have time to play.

Reggie: I'm really happy about that! It's in my bedroom. I'll go and get it!

Dad: Oh, and don't forget the [4] **cords** / **engines** / **steers** for our smartphones.

Mom: Is everyone ready?

Dad: Oh, no! The [5] **propeller** / **engine** / **glider** won't start.

Mom: Hmm. Maybe the [6] **motor** / **basketball** / **glider** isn't working. I'll call Uncle Dwayne. He can help!

B Find the adjectives with prepositions in **A**. Underline the adjectives. Circle the prepositions.

C Write the questions and sentences. Add the correct preposition after the adjective.

1 ____ (you / interested / pocket watches / ?)

2 ____ (she / curious / how the motor works / .)

3 ____ (they / good / surfing / ?)

4 ____ (he / happy / the new basketball / .)

Unit 15 and Me

How hard I worked ☆☆☆☆☆   Did I reach my goal?   

One thing I learned is ____ .

My goal for Unit 16 is ____ .

Vocabulary 1

A Complete the sentences.

> meadow   graze   midday   rock   piece   wolf

1 Cows and sheep ______________ on grass.

2 I'm tired. Let's sit on that ______________ for a moment.

3 Look at the wildflowers in the ______________.

4 That's not a big dog. It's a ______________!

5 Can I have a ______________ of pizza, please?

6 We always eat lunch at ______________.

B Circle *True* or *False*.

1 Some olives are green and some are black.   True   False

2 Peaches grow under the ground.   True   False

3 Nuts are healthy and have protein.   True   False

4 Figs are fruit. They grow on trees.   True   False

What do you usually do at midday?

A Match the questions and answers.

1 Would you like to try some figs?

2 Would you like to hike on that trail?

3 Would you like a piece of cake?

4 Would you like some water?

5 Would you like to leave at midday?

a No, I wouldn't. It's too hot to walk outside.

b Yes, please. I'm thirsty.

c Yes, I would. They look delicious!

d No, thanks. It's too sweet for me.

e No, I wouldn't. That's too late. Can we leave earlier?

B Complete the dialogues.

Would you like   Would you like   I'd like to walk   No, thanks
I'd like to sit   please   Would you like to   Would you like to

1 A: ______________________ sit on the rock with me?

B: Yes, ______________________ there.

2 A: ______________________ walk to that meadow?

B: Yes, ______________________ there.

3 A: ______________________ some more nuts?

B: ______________________ .

4 B: ______________________ a peach?

A: Yes, ______________________ . I'm getting hungry!

 Unscramble the words to make questions.

1 Would / like / you / eat / ? / lunch / to / now

____

____

2 like / ? / some / Would / you / water

____

____

3 to watch TV / you / ? / like / Would

____

____

4 my camera / Would / like / you / ? / to borrow

____

____

5 Would / like / ? / a piece / you / of that pizza

____

____

D **Check (✓) the answers to the questions in C.**

1 ☐ **a** Yes, I would. ☐ **b** No, thanks!

2 ☐ **a** Yes, I would. ☐ **b** No, thanks!

3 ☐ **a** Yes, I would. ☐ **b** No, thanks!

4 ☐ **a** Yes, I would. ☐ **b** No, thanks!

5 ☐ **a** Yes, I would. ☐ **b** No, thanks!

Would you like pizza with olives for lunch?

A **Read the informational story. What do wolves like to eat?**

FREYA THE WOLF

Nils is nine years old, and he loves all animals. Yesterday, he saw a video about a man who had a wolf called Freya as a pet. The wolf wasn't healthy. So, the man called the New Paws Wolf Sanctuary for help. They took Freya to live there.

"Mom," Nils asked, "Why did they take Freya away?"

"We can't keep wild animals as pets. In a house, a wolf can't eat the right food, and they can't exercise well. It may get sick or have low energy. It's not good for them," his mom Marit explained.

"Is Freya going to be OK?" asked Nils worriedly.

"I hope so, but I really don't know," answered his mom sadly.

"Are you still worried about Freya?" Nils' mom asked. Nils nodded. "OK, I'll try to find out some information, but it's time to go now."

At midday, Marit called the New Paws Wolf Sanctuary. She spoke to a man named Erik. She asked him about Freya. He told her that Freya was getting stronger and healthier every day.

"Would you like to come and visit?" Erik asked kindly.

"Yes, we would!" said Marit. "My son will be so happy. Thank you!"

That night, Marit told Nils about the invitation. He hugged his mom. The next weekend, they went to the wolf park.

"We cannot touch the animals, but we can watch them from here," explained Erik.

"Which one is Freya?" asked Marit.

"Do you see the one standing on that big rock?" Erik pointed towards the meadow.

"Yes, she looks happy," said Marit.

"Would you like to ask any questions?" asked Erik.

"What does Freya eat?" asked Nils.

Erik replied, "Wolves are carnivores, so they eat meat. In the wild, they hunt animals like rabbits. Here, we give them fresh meat. They also catch rabbits in the forest. Wolves eat about nine kilograms of food every day!"

"Do they eat anything else?"

"Yes, they like fruit, vegetables, and grass, too."

"Why do they eat so much?"

Erik replied, "They eat a lot because they are very active. They use a lot of energy running, jumping, and playing."

"That's good," said Nils. "These wolves are safe and happy. That makes me happy, too!"

B Underline these words in the text.

wolf   midday   rock   meadow

C Write the correct answer.

1 How did Nils first hear about Freya? _______________________

2 How did Marit get more information about Freya? _______________________

3 Where did Erik invite Nils and Marit? _______________________

4 Where does Erik work? _______________________

5 How did they know the wolves were happy? _______________________

D Circle *True* or *False*.

1 People can keep wolves as pets.   True   False

2 Wolves are carnivores.   True   False

3 Wolves eat two kilograms of food each day.   True   False

4 Wolves eat a lot because they are active.   True   False

E  Write three questions about wolves or wolf parks in your notebook. Use the question words to help you.

Who   What   Where   When   Why

A **Complete the sentences with the correct words.**

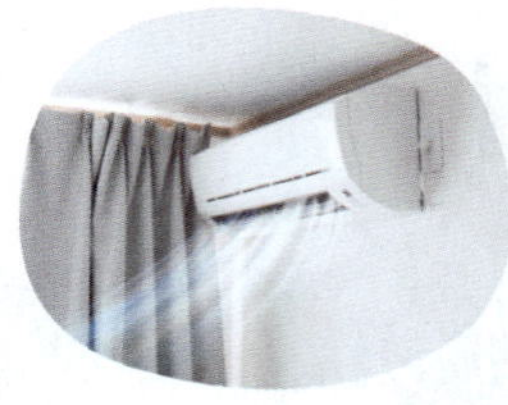

1 The new a __ __ c __ __ d __ __ __ o __ __ __
cools the house quickly.

2 I have a lot of dirty clothes to put in the
w __ __ h __ __ __ __ __ a __ __ __ n __ .

3 What's cooking on the __ __ __ v __ ?

4 The TV won't turn on because there's no
e __ __ __ __ r __ __ __ __ y.

5 Planes and cars are made of m __ t __ __ .

6 Use __ __ o __ __ p __ __ __ e and a toothbrush
to clean your teeth.

7 What kind of __ r __ __ __ __ p __ __ __ __ a __ __ __ n
is common in your city?

8 Do you keep eggs in the r __ f __ __ g __ __ a __ __ __ ?

B **Write *True* if the sentence is true. Correct the false sentences.**

1 We clean our clothes in the **refrigerator**.   washing machine

2 Cars and buses are types of **transportation**.   ___________________

3 These knives and forks are made of **toothpaste**.   ___________________

4 When it's hot, we turn on the **stove**.   ___________________

5 The lights and the TV use **electricity**.   ___________________

6 We usually put the milk in the **washing machine**.   ___________________

What things in your home use electricity?

A **Circle the correct option.**

1 These … vegetables and chicken are delicious!

   a grilled   **b** donut   **c** bowl

2 I love eating a sweet, round … .

   a gecko   **b** string   **c** donut

3 A … is a kind of lizard.

   a flute   **b** gecko   **c** donut

4 I use a … for my breakfast cereal in the morning.

   a bowl   **b** flute   **c** string

5 We can tie this package up with … .

   a donuts   **b** geckos   **c** string

6 Can you play the … ?

   a gecko   **b** flute   **c** string

B **Match the pictures with the sentences in A.**

A **Think about what happens first and second. Complete the sentences with _before_ or _after_.**

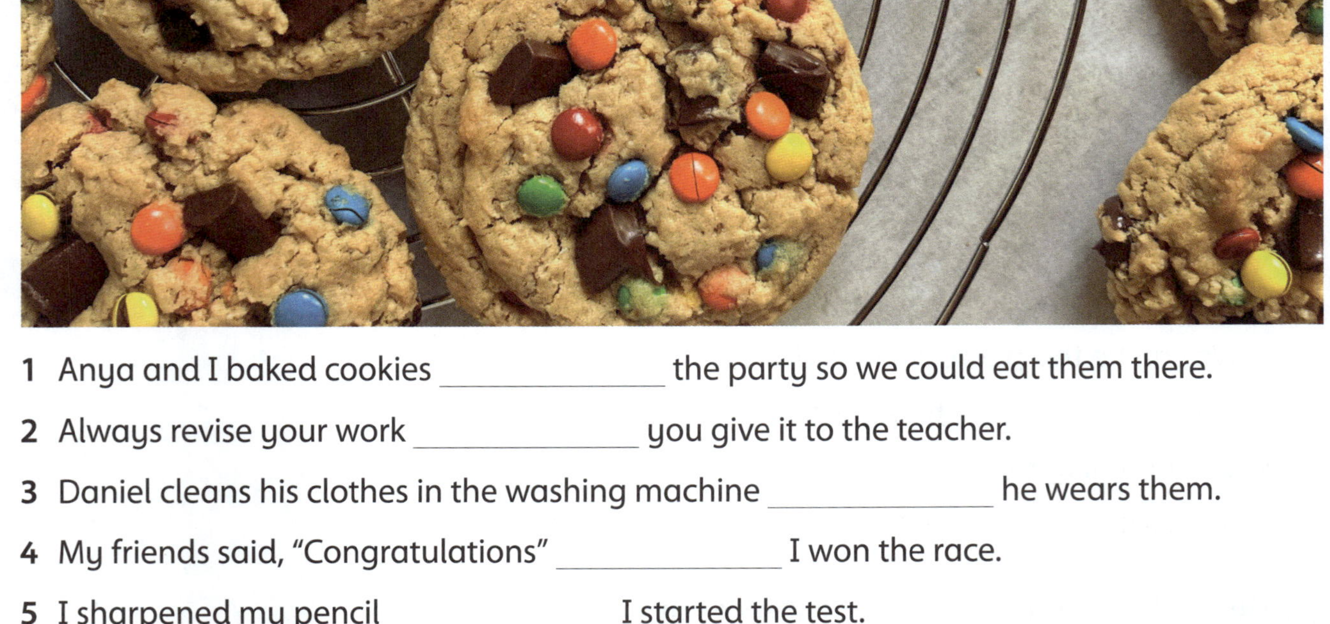

1 Anya and I baked cookies _______________ the party so we could eat them there.

2 Always revise your work _______________ you give it to the teacher.

3 Daniel cleans his clothes in the washing machine _______________ he wears them.

4 My friends said, "Congratulations" _______________ I won the race.

5 I sharpened my pencil _______________ I started the test.

B **Combine the sentences using _before_ and _after_. Write one new sentence with _before_ and one new sentence with _after_.**

1 We arrived at school. We started class.

   a We arrived at school before we started class. _______________

   b ____

2 She brushed her teeth. She went to bed.

   a ____

   b ____

3 He borrowed money from me. He bought lunch.

   a ____

   b ____

4 My dad bought vegetables. He grilled them.

   a ____

   b ____

C **In your notebook, write about something you did that used energy. Use at least two complex sentences with _before_ and _after_.**

A **Check (✓) all the correct options.**

1 Things that use electricity

☐ washing machine ☐ flute ☐ refrigerator ☐ air conditioner

2 Animals

☐ donut ☐ gecko ☐ wolf ☐ string

3 Things you can eat

☐ olive ☐ peach ☐ nuts ☐ metal

4 Things in the kitchen

☐ bowl ☐ transportation ☐ stove ☐ refrigerator

5 Things in nature

☐ meadow ☐ rock ☐ electricity ☐ toothpaste

B **Write questions using *Would you like*.**

1 _______________________________ ? (a donut)

2 _______________________________

_______________________________ ? (to run in the meadow together)

3 _______________________________ ? (some nuts)

4 _______________________________ ?

(to pick peaches with me)

5 _______________________________ ? (a piece of pie)

Unit 16 and Me

How hard I worked ☆☆☆☆☆   Did I reach my goal? ☺ ☺ ☹

One thing I learned is _______________________________ .

My goal for Unit 17 is _______________________________ .

17 How does energy affect people's lives?

A Complete the sentences with the correct words.

1 Our kitchen stove uses n __ __ __ r __ __ g __ __ to cook food.

2 Pollution is not good for the Earth's __ __ m __ __ __ h __ __ e.

3 O __ __ is found underground. It is sticky and black.

4 The p __ w __ __ __ p __ __ __ __ __ near our house makes electricity.

B Complete the text.

> coal   gasoline   fuel   smog   steam CO_2

Last weekend, my family went on a trip. Our car needed **1** _______________, and so did we. We filled the car with **2** _______________ and then stopped for lunch. After that, we drove out of the city. I was happy to leave the **3** _______________ from the city behind and breathe the fresh country air. On the first day, we visited a train museum. Did you know old trains burned **4** _______________ to make **5** _______________ to power the train's engine? On the second day, we visited a big garden. We learned that the green color in trees and plants is connected to how plants turn **6** _______________ into oxygen. We bought a plant to take home. Maybe the city air will be a little cleaner!

A **Read. Number the pictures to match the sentences.**

1 The train is going through the tunnel.

2 The train is going into the station.

3 The train is going across the bridge.

4 The train is going around the lake.

B **Complete the poster. You will use some words more than once.**

across   into   through   around

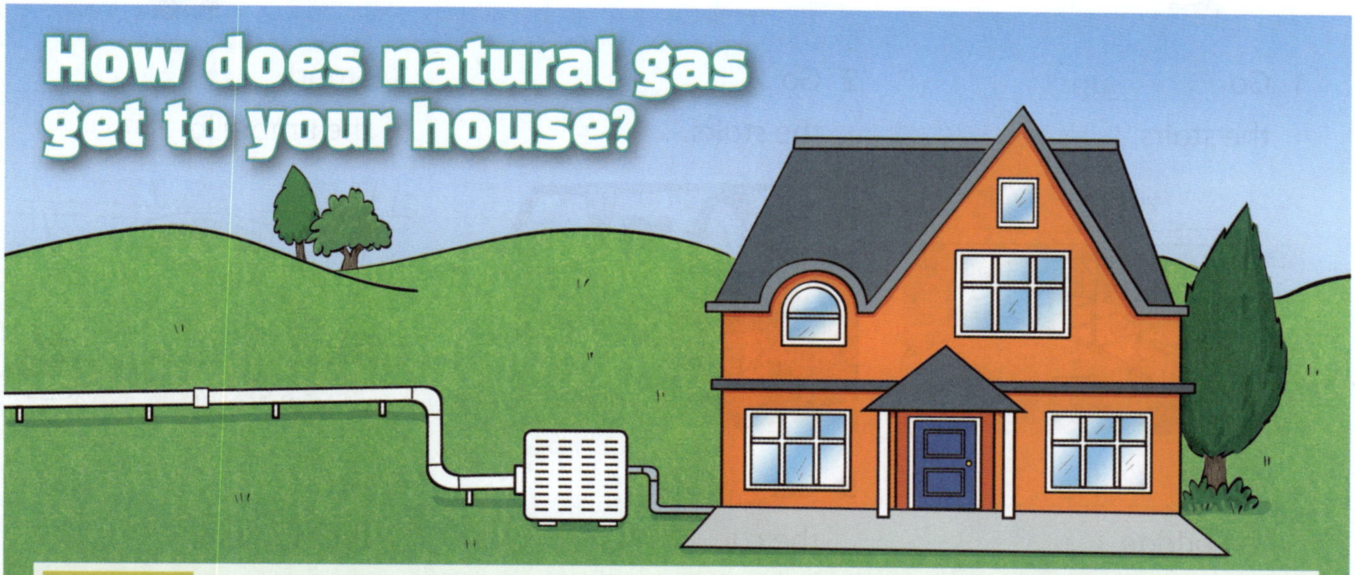

How does natural gas get to your house?

STEP 1: The gas company drills ______________ the earth to get the gas.

STEP 2: The company sends the gas ______________ many kilometers ______________ big underground pipes.

STEP 3: Then the gas goes ______________ smaller pipes and ______________ your home.

STEP 4: The pipes in your house send the gas ______________ your house, so you can use it for heating and cooking.

C Match the opposites.

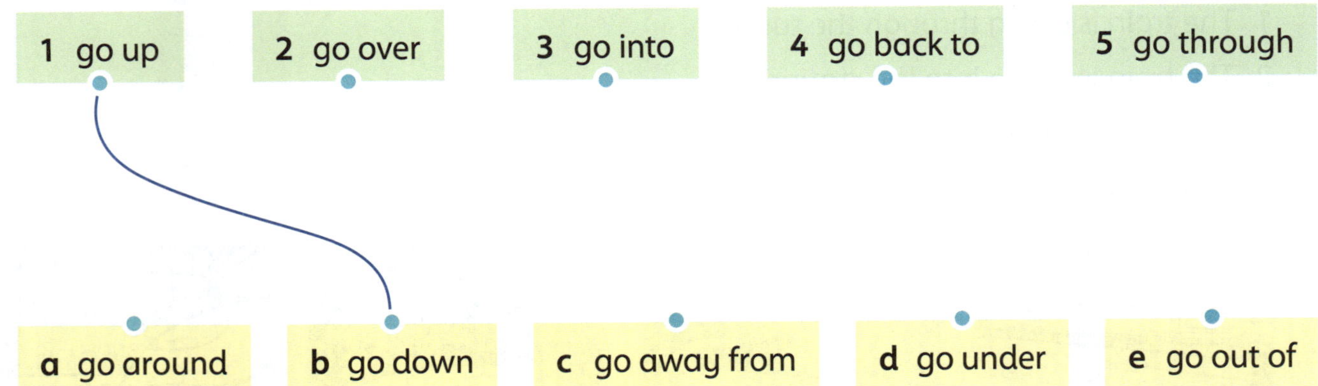

D Give directions for each picture using the prepositions in **C**. Two are not used.

1 Go _____ up _____ the stairs.

2 Go _____________ the stairs.

3 Stand _____________ the umbrella.

4 Walk _____________ the bridge.

5 Get _____________ the car.

6 Go _____________ the stadium.

7 Walk _____________ the gymnasium.

8 Run _____________ the lake.

A Read the science magazine article. How does the author feel about smog?

Smog in the Air

Where does the word *smog* come from? It takes the *sm* from *smoke* and adds it to the *og* from *fog*. People first used this word in the early 1900s! But what is smog, and why does it happen?

Smog is a kind of air pollution. It first happened because the smoke from burning coal mixed with the air. This made it hard to see and breathe. Now, smog also comes from cars, factories, and power plants. Burning gasoline, oil, and even trash can create smog. It happens when the sunlight mixes with tiny particles in the air, like CO_2. Hot temperatures make this worse.

Smog is harmful for people and animals, especially children and people with breathing problems or lung diseases. Smog can hurt the lungs and make it difficult to breathe. It is harmful for plants, too. Smog can hurt or kill plants. Smog can even damage buildings and cars.

Many cities around the world have smog. Sometimes, where a city is located makes the smog problem worse. For example, in cities with mountains around them, the smog gets stuck because the wind can't blow it away.

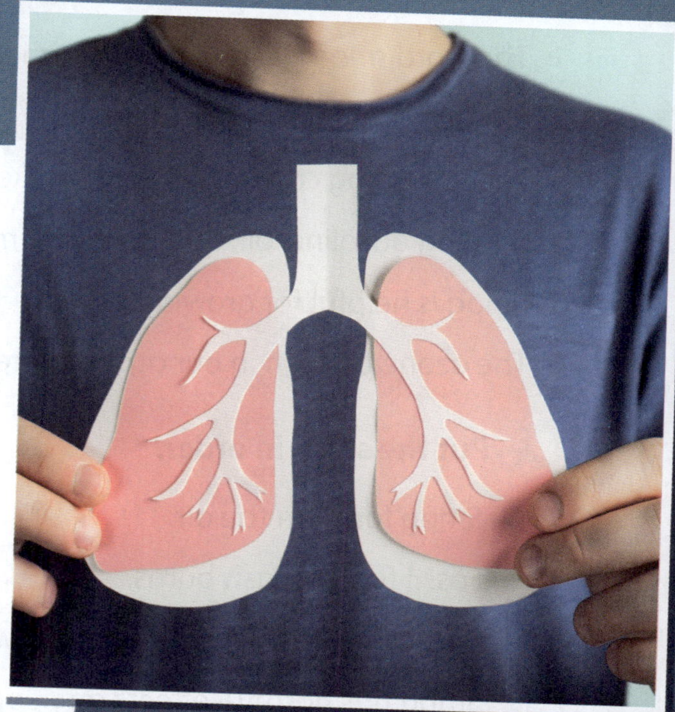

B Underline these words in the text.

smog   coal   power plants
gasoline CO_2 oil   atmosphere

C Write *True* or *False*.

1 The word *smog* is a mix of *smoke* and *frog*. ______________

2 Smog is a kind of air pollution. ______________

3 The first smog came from coal smoke in the air. ______________

4 Burning gasoline, oil, and trash can make smog. ______________

5 Smog is helpful for growing plants. ______________

6 The ozone up high in our atmosphere is helpful. ______________

D Put the steps in order.

______ Smog forms in the air.

______ Fossil fuel or trash burns.

______ Particles go into the air and mix with sunlight.

______ Smog has harmful effects on people, animals, and plants.

A Circle the correct option.

1 The **windmill** / **hydroelectric plant** / **sailboat** uses water to make energy for our town. A **blade** / **battery** / **dam** holds the water back.

2 **Wind turbines** / **Solar panels** / **Batteries** only work when it's windy. The wind makes the **sailboat** / **blades** / **dam** turn, and it creates energy.

3 **Dams** / **Solar panels** / **Wind turbines** don't work when the sun isn't shining. But **batteries** / **dams** / **blades** store energy that the sun created.

B Complete the text.

motor   blades   sailboat   windmills

Last weekend, my uncle and I went to a beautiful lake, and we took a ride in his
¹ _______________ . It did not have an engine or a ² _______________ , and it did not use gasoline. It was amazing to move across the water with wind powering the sails. We went by a farm and saw several ³ _______________ . The ⁴ _______________ were turning slowly in the wind. It was so cool to see them up close!

Where can you see solar panels or wind turbines in your country?

A **Number the pictures to match the sentences.**

1 When it's cold outside, the furnace keeps us warm inside.

2 My cousin takes medicine for asthma every day.

3 The hiking trail goes through a nice wooded area in the forest.

4 I'm using a pattern and a sewing machine to make this new shirt.

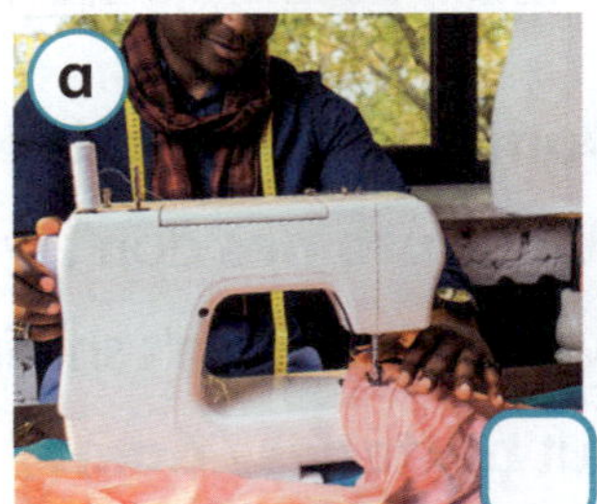

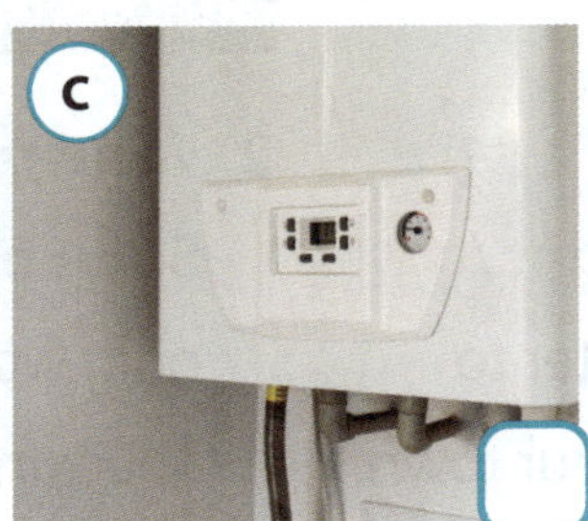

B **Complete the dialogues.**

plug it in   charge   sewing machine   asthma   furnace   wooded

1 **A:** Where can I ___________________ my phone?

B: You can ___________________ over there.

2 **A:** Did you enjoy your hike through that ___________________ area?

B: Not really. I couldn't breathe very well because of my ___________________.

3 **A:** It's so cold! Is the ___________________ working now?

B: Yes, we just fixed it.

4 **A:** Can you fix this hole in my shirt?

B: Sure. Bring it here, and I'll use the ___________________.

What things do you plug in?

A Read the biography. Then label its parts.

Introduction   Childhood and education   Achievements   Conclusion

Dr. Mária Telkes: The Sun Queen

1 People started using the sun's energy a long time ago. Dr. Mária Telkes became a scientist to discover more about how to use the sun's energy.

2 Dr. Telkes was born in Hungary in 1900. She studied chemistry in Hungary before she moved to the United States in 1925. In 1939, she started working on solar energy projects.

3 Dr. Telkes wanted to design a home that used only solar energy. In the 1940s, she worked with architect Eleanor Raymond. They created a house that used the sun for heat. She also invented a solar oven. People could use it anywhere. In 1953, Dr. Telkes won the first Society of Women Engineers Achievement Award.

4 Mária Telkes lived to be 95 years old. She invented over 20 things, and most of them used solar power. Her work helped make using the sun's energy popular.

B Choose a scientist or an inventor. Research their life. Write notes for a biography.

Name	
Where and when born	
Childhood	
Education	
Achievements	

C Use your notes from **B** to write a biography in your notebook.

D Check your writing. Use the checklist on page 176 to help you.

A Three of the four are correct. Cross out (*X*) the wrong option.

1 **Kinds of energy:**

  a coal   **b** asthma   **c** natural gas   **d** oil

2 **Things that make energy:**

  a power plant   **b** wind turbine   **c** sewing machine   **d** hydroelectric plant

3 **Things related to the air:**

  a atmosphere   **b** smog   **c** CO_2 **d** furnace

4 **Things related to water:**

  a wooded   **b** steam   **c** dam   **d** sailboat

B Unscramble the words in parentheses to complete the sentences.

When ¹ c______________ (ocal) and ² o______________ (loi) burn, they make ³ C______________ (O_2C). This goes into the ⁴ a______________ (moaephrtse) and causes ⁵ s______________ (msog).

A ⁶ s______________ (lbosatia) uses wind power to move across the water. Wind also moves the ⁷ b______________ (dlabes) of ⁸ w______________ t______________ (dwin tbrniuse). Then, the energy goes into ⁹ b______________ (ttbseiare) for people to use.

C Complete sentences with *across, around, into,* or *through.*

1 Steam-powered ships and trucks transport oil ______________ the world.

2 Gasoline goes ______________ a pipe into your car's motor.

3 Wires help electricity come ______________ your house.

4 A dam stops water because it goes ______________ a river.

Unit 17 and Me

How hard I worked ☆☆☆☆☆   Did I reach my goal? ☺ ☺ ☹

One thing I learned is ______________________________.

My goal for Unit 18 is ______________________________.

Vocabulary 1

A Unscramble the words in parentheses to complete the sentences.

1 The teacher told us to be s____________ (lisent) in the library.

2 Use this t____________ (wotel) after you swim.

3 I cook spaghetti in this big p____________ (otp).

4 Is this the right l____________ (ldi) for that jar?

B Number the pictures to match the sentences in **A**.

C Complete the text.

> degrees   dryer   electric fan   heat wave   outage   clothesline

We're having a ¹ ____________ this week. It will be 40 ² ____________ Celsius tomorrow. After you wash the clothes, don't put them in the ³ ____________. Hang them on a ⁴ ____________ outside. After that, don't use the air conditioner if you want to keep cool. Use the ⁵ ____________. If we use too much electricity, we might have a power ⁶ ____________!

How do you stay cool in a heat wave?

A Circle *want to*, *need to*, or *have to* to complete the sentences.

1 Bella and Cassie **want to** / **need to** go swimming this afternoon.

2 All the students **want to** / **need to** bring their lunch on the field trip. There's no cafeteria.

3 Grant **wants to** / **needs to** eat chocolate cake for dessert.

4 We **want to** / **need to** save as much energy as possible.

5 Chariya **wants to** / **has to** do her homework before she watches TV.

6 I **want to** / **have to** wear tennis shoes to play tennis.

B Read and check (✓) the correct answer.

1 Does he want to eat ice cream?

☐ Yes, he does.　☐ No, he doesn't.

2 Does she want to save energy?

☐ Yes, she does.　☐ No, she doesn't.

3 Did he need to study hard?

☐ Yes, he did.　☐ No, he didn't.

4 Did she have to practice soccer every day this week?

☐ Yes, she did.　☐ No, she didn't.

 Complete the questions. Then write the answers.

1 ___Do they need to use___ the electric fan? (they / need to / use)

✓ _______________________________

2 _______________________ in the pool? (she / want to / swim)

✓ _______________________________

3 _______________________ his homework? (he / want to / do)

✗ _______________________________

4 _______________________ his phone? (he / have to / charge)

✓ _______________________________

 Unscramble the questions. Then write the answers.

1 What / do / ? / have to / every day / does / Liam

A: _______________________________

B: _______________________________

2 Olivia and Caleb / on the weekend / want to / do / What do / ?

A: _______________________________

B: _______________________________

3 we / need to / What do / ? / electricity / do / to save

A: _______________________________

B: _______________________________

A Read the humorous story. How are the two characters different?

THE POWER'S OUT!

Dana Brown and Victor Green were best friends. They went to the same school. They lived in the same building. They did almost everything together.

One day, Dana and Victor were walking home from school when it started snowing.

"What's the opposite of a heat wave?" asked Victor.

"Hmm. It's a cold snap!" replied Dana.

"OK. Then we're having a cold snap. *Brrr*!" said Victor.

"Ha! Bye, Victor," said Dana.

"Bye!"

Victor opened the front door to his apartment. "Hi, I'm home!" he said. "Ooh, it's nice and warm in here."

Dana walked into her kitchen. Her parents were washing dishes by hand. "Hi, Mom and Dad!" she said.

Victor was drying his hair when the power suddenly went out. Everything was silent. The apartment was dark. "Mom! What happened?"

"The power is out," she replied. "It's not just us. It's the whole building!"

"I'm scared," said Ana, Victor's little sister.

"It's OK," Victor said. "What do we need to do?"

"Let's check on the Browns," said Victor's mom. "The electricity will come back on soon. Here, take your coats with you … and Power's blanket."

Victor, Ana, Ms. Green, and Power went next door. Mr. Brown opened the door. "Come in! Come in!" said Mrs. Brown. "We can get through this outage together. Are you hungry? We made a big pot of soup."

"It will warm us up and give us energy," said Mr. Brown. "Then we can play some board games."

"Thank you," said Ms. Green.

"Board games? I want to play video games," suggested Dana.

"But we can't play video games without power," said Victor.

"Meow!?" said Power, hearing his name.

"Oh, right!" said Dana.

After a few hours, the electricity came back on. Everyone looked up and cheered.

"The power's back!" said Ana.

"Meow!" said Power.

Everyone laughed.

"Let's finish our game!" said Mr. Brown, and everyone agreed.

Victor said, "Wait! I need to do something first."

Victor ran home and turned off the TV and the hair dryer. Then he turned off the laptop and the tablet. After that he turned the heat down to 20 degrees. Finally, he grabbed Power's little cat sweater and turned off the lights.

Victor returned to the Browns' apartment. With a smile, he asked, "OK, whose turn is it?"

B **Underline these words in the text.**

heat wave   silent   outage   pot   hair dryer   degrees

C **Answer the questions.**

1 What's the weather like in the story? ___________________

2 What temperature was the Greens' apartment at the end? ___________________

3 What did the Greens do when the power went out? ___________________

4 Why couldn't they play video games? ___________________

5 What did Victor do when the power came back on? ___________________

D **Can you make these inferences? Circle *True* or *False*.**

1 Both families can control the temperatures in their apartments.   True   False

2 The Greens use more electricity than the Browns.   True   False

3 The Browns and the Greens were good friends.   True   False

4 Power was an unfriendly cat.   True   False

5 Victor learned to be more careful about energy.   True   False

A **Circle the correct option.**

Our city is very green. There are a lot of **¹ offshore / heat / charging stations** for electric cars. You only need to drive a few **² kilometers / vines / lanes** to find one. At night, our city uses **³ dim / lane / vine** street lights to save energy. Right now, my family is driving home on a busy **⁴ dim / charging station / highway**. It has four **⁵ vines / lanes / kilometers**. Look, there's our house! We painted it white to **⁶ reflect / dim / offshore** the light.

B **Complete the sentences.**

> dim   kilometers   vines   heat

1 Our house is covered with lots of green __________ .

2 It is hard to read when the lights in my room are __________ .

3 The race is ten __________ long.

4 Remember to drink a lot of water in the __________ .

About how many kilometers is your home from your school?

A **Replace the underlined words with the correct words.**

1 There's a power outage, so we need to use a <u>cardboard</u> for electricity.

____

2 Boxes are usually made of strong <u>raspberries</u>.

____

3 We wrapped the leftover food in <u>cabbage</u>.

____

4 We're making <u>generator</u> soup for dinner.

____

5 When a <u>blueberry</u> turns red, you can pick and eat it.

____

6 I like to make <u>aluminum foil</u> pancakes on the weekend.

____

B **Complete the conversation.**   blueberry   raspberry   aluminum foil   cardboard

Lisa: Hi! Welcome to our bake sale.

Ben: Would you like to buy a pie or some ¹ _______________ muffins?

Ms. Lal: I'll take six muffins, please. Can you wrap them in ² _______________ ?

Ben: Yes, here you are.

Ms. Lal: Can I have a ³ _______________ pie, too, please?

Lisa: Sure! I'll put the pie in a ⁴ _______________ box, so it's easier to carry.

Ms. Lal: Thank you!

A **Read the sentences. Circle the nouns. Underline the verbs.**

1 My parents <u>work</u> from 9:00 to 5:00. Their (work) is interesting.

2 What did they <u>name</u> their kitten? Is its name Mittens?

3 I can't <u>pedal</u> up the hill. The pedal is broken.

4 I usually <u>answer</u> questions in class, but I don't know the answer to number 4.

5 The <u>paint</u> in your room is really nice. I want to paint my room the same color.

6 I left a <u>message</u> on my grandma's phone. I'll message her again later.

B **Complete the sentences. Then write *noun* or *verb*.**

~~drink~~   cooks   joke   color   play   walk

1 Would you like a _____drink_____ of water? _____noun_____

2 My dad _____________ dinner on Tuesdays, Thursdays, and Saturdays. _____________

3 Which _____________ do you like better: green or blue? _____________

4 Do you like to _____________ on the swings or the seesaw at the park? _____________

5 In the afternoon, I go for a _____________ around the lake near my house. _____________

C **Write five new sentences with the words from B in your notebook. Use the nouns as verbs and the verbs as nouns.**

A **Two of the three options are correct. Cross out (X) the wrong option.**

1 **Measurements:**   a kilometer   b degree   c towel

2 **Things on a stove:**   a clothesline   b pot   c lid

3 **Things you use to clean clothes:**   a cabbage   b washing machine   c dryer

4 **Related to weather:**   a degree   b silent   c heat wave

5 **Things you use on a road trip:**   a highway   b vine   c charging station

B **Complete the text with *need to*, *have to*, or *want to*.**

Tomorrow is my mom's birthday. I **1** ______________ make a raspberry cake for her! First, I **2** ______________ get the ingredients, like flour, eggs, and butter. Then, I **3** ______________ check the fridge for raspberries. I'll ask my little sister if she **4** ______________ help. Next, I **5** ______________ turn on the oven. When the cake is finished, I **6** ______________ ask my dad to help me turn off the oven. We **7** ______________ be careful because it's hot, but we don't **8** ______________ waste electricity.

C **Write the questions and answers.**

1 A: ______________________________________ ?

(they / have to / wear boots in the snow)

B: Yes, ______________ .

2 A: ______________________________________ ?

(he / need to / turn off the light)

B: Yes, ______________ .

3 A: ______________________________________ ?

(they / want to / watch TV)

B: No, ______________ . They ______________ turn on the fan.

Unit 18 and Me

How hard I worked ☆☆☆☆☆   Did I reach my goal? ☺ 😐 ☹

One thing I learned is ____ .

My goal for next year is ____ .

Grammar Reference

Unit 1

Grammar: Gerund

A **gerund** uses the **-ing** form of a verb to act as a noun. (**spend → spending**)

We can use gerunds as the **subject** or the **object** of a sentence.

Spending time with my pets helps my well-being.

I love spending time with my grandmother.

We use gerunds after verbs for **likes** or **dislikes**, such as *love, like, enjoy, hate,* or *prefer*. We also use them after phrases with an adjective + preposition, such as *good at, scared of, bad at, interested in, worried about,* or *bored with*.

Circle the correct option.

1 **Play** / **Playing** tennis keeps me healthy.

2 **Eat** / **Eating** well is good for my body.

3 My mom enjoys **watch** / **watching** movies with us.

Unit 2

Grammar: Can and Could

We use **can** + verb to talk about things we are able to do in the present. We use **can't** + verb for things we are <u>not</u> able to do.

She can speak Japanese well. / She can't speak Arabic.

Can she speak Japanese well? Yes, she can. / No, she can't.

We use **could** + verb to talk about things we were able to do in the past. We use **couldn't** + verb for things we were <u>not</u> able to do.

She couldn't speak Japanese when she arrived in Japan.

Could she speak Japanese? Yes, she could. / No, she couldn't.

Can and **could** don't change form.

Complete the sentences with *can, can't, could,* or *couldn't*.

1 He ______________ ride a bike when he was four, but now he ______________ ride a bike.

2 A: ______________ Jimena swim well when she was five?

B: No, she ______________, but she ______________ now!

Unit 3

Adjectives with *-ed* and *-ing*

We use **adjectives** to describe nouns. Adjectives that end in **-ed** tell us about a person's feelings. Adjectives that end in **-ing** tell us about an action or a thing.

excited I was excit**ed** to watch the soccer game.

exciting The soccer game was excit**ing**!

Circle the correct option.

1 I'm really **interested** / **interesting** in sharks and whales.

2 The ending of the superhero movie was **surprised** / **surprising** .

3 Waiting at the doctor's office is **bored** / **boring** .

Unit 4

Zero Conditional

We use the **zero conditional** to talk about an event and the result of the event.

The **if-clause** starts with **if** or **when**. The **main clause** gives the result of the if-clause. When the *if*-clause is first, add a **comma** (,) after it.

If it rains,   **the children stay in school.**

if-clause   main clause

You can change the order of the clauses. **Don't** use a comma when the result is first.

The children stay in school   **if** it rains.

    main clause   **if**-clause

In your notebook, combine the sentences using the zero conditional. Then switch the clauses and write again.

1 The children water the plants. The plants grow bigger.

When the children water the plants, the plants grow bigger.

The plants grow bigger when the children water the plants.

2 We help the Earth. We have a healthy planet.

3 The gardener brings seeds. The volunteers plant them.

Unit 5

Grammar: Past Continuous

We use the **past continuous** to talk about things that **were happening** at a certain time in the past. We use *was* or *were* + a verb ending in *-ing*.

She **was playing** tennis. They **were singing**.

He **wasn't playing** tennis. You **weren't singing**.

Was she **playing** tennis? Yes, she was. / No, she wasn't.

Were they **singing**? Yes, they were. / No, they weren't.

What **were** they **doing** yesterday? They **were playing** in the park.

Spelling

agree + *-ing*
= agreeing

ride ~~e~~ + *-ing*
= riding

tie ~~ie~~ + y + *-ing*
= tying

Complete the sentences and questions using the past continuous.

1 Yesterday afternoon, they _______________ (shop) at the mall.

2 **A:** What _______________ the puppets _______________ (do) ?
   B: They _______________ (ride) horses.

3 **A:** _______________ the children _______________ (watch)
      the show?
   B: Yes, they _______________ .

Unit 6

Grammar: Past Continuous and Simple Past

We use the **past continuous** and the **simple past** in the same sentence to talk about two things that happened during the same time. We use the **simple past** to talk about the interrupting action and *when* to connect the two actions.

My sister was watching TV when I went to bed last night.

The two parts of the sentence can change places. We use a **comma** (,) when the simple past is first.

When I went to bed last night, my sister was watching TV.

In your notebook, combine the sentences with *when*. Then put the simple past first and write again.

1 We were learning about composting. The bell rang.

2 The children were interviewing the gardener. It started to rain.

3 Ali and Cana were volunteering at the school fair. The principal arrived.

Unit 7

Grammar: Future Plans with *Going to*

We use *going to* + verb to talk about future plans.

I'm / She's / They're going to write to my / her / their cousin.

I'm / He's / We're not going to call my / his / our cousin.

Are you / Is he / Are they going to talk to the teacher?

Yes, I am / he is / they are. / No, I'm not / he isn't / they aren't.

When we use *going to*, we only change the form of *be*.

I'm / He's / They're going to work hard this year.

Complete the sentences and questions with *going to*.

1 A: _____________ he _____________ (play) basketball?

   B: Yes, _____________ .

2 They _____________ (sit) together at lunch.

3 We _____________ (visit) our grandmother this weekend.

4 A: _____________ you _____________ (take) his advice?

   B: No, _____________ .

Unit 8

Grammar: Future Facts with *Will*

We use *will* + verb to talk about future facts. We don't change the form of the verb after *will*.

We / They will wake up at seven o'clock tomorrow.

They will be here at ten o'clock.

She won't be here at ten o'clock.

Will you be here at ten o'clock?

Unscramble the sentences in your notebook. 

1 come / in a superhero costume / . / She / will

2 will / They / . / traditional costumes / wear

3 10:00 a.m. / . / will / The event / start at

4 end / at 1:00 p.m. / The event / . / will

Unit 9

We use *may* or *might* + verb if we are not sure about the future. If we are sure, we use *will* or *won't* + verb. We don't change the form of the verb after *may* and *might*.

Clubs Day will be on Friday. (We are sure this will happen.)

A lot of students might join clubs. (We are not sure this will happen.)

He won't join the drama club. (We are sure this won't happen.)

He might not join the drama club. (We are not sure if this will happen.)

Rewrite the future facts as possibilities in your notebook using *may* and *might*. 

1 She will write in her journal tonight.

2 He won't get up early tomorrow.

3 I will invite my friend to my house this Saturday.

4 They will take the train home in the morning.

Unit 10

We use *a few* to talk about things we can count.

There were a few birds in the yard today.

We use *a little* to talk about things we cannot count.

Put only a little sugar in the cake.

We use *a lot of* or *lots of* to talk about things we can and cannot count.

I saw a lot of animals at the safari park.

There is lots of water in the lake.

Complete the sentences with *a few*, *a little*, *a lot of*, or *lots of*.

1 I saw _____________ butterflies today. There were just two or three.

2 There are _____________ birds in the flock. There may be hundreds of them!

3 The plants need _____________ water. Use just a small cup.

4 There were _____________ ants at the picnic. I couldn't count them all!

Unit 11

Grammar: Comparative and Superlative Adjectives

We use **comparative adjectives** to compare two people or things. Use **-er + than** for short adjectives. Use **more** for long adjectives.

My bedroom is cleaner than my brother's. My room is more organized than his.

Use **superlative adjectives** to compare three or more people or things. Use **the + -est** for short adjectives. Use **the most** for long adjectives.

Our school is the biggest in the city. It's the most modern in the city.

Complete the chart.

Adjective	Comparative	Superlative
I'm **young**.	I'm [1] younger than my brother.	I'm [2] ___________ person in my family.
The computer is **expensive**.	It's [3] ___________ the tablet.	It's [4] ___________ item in the store.
Karla's pencil case is **colorful**.	It's [5] ___________ mine.	Karla's pencil case is [6] ___________ in the class.

Unit 12

Grammar: Comparative Adjectives with As

We use **as + adjective + as** to compare two people or things that are *similar*.

Emily is as old as Zoe.

We use **not as + adjective + as** to compare two people or things that are *different*.

Mice are not as loud as birds.

Complete the sentences with (*not*) as + adjective + as.

1 The strawberry is ___________ (not big) the orange.

2 Ken is ___________ (tall) Ibrahim.

3 Liz's poem is ___________ (not long) Laura's.

4 The parrot is ___________ (colorful) the butterfly.

Unit 13

We use **too** to agree with positive statements.

A ger is round. An igloo is, too.

We use **either** in a sentence to agree with negative statements.

Turf houses didn't have running water. Castles didn't, either.

We use **too** and **either** after a **comma** (**,**) at the end of a sentence.

Match.

1 I'd like to visit a ger.	**a** I'd like to visit one, too.
2 Caro doesn't want to stay in the castle.	**b** I didn't like it, either.
3 Our school has a courtyard.	**c** Jun doesn't, either.
4 Fareed didn't like the movie.	**d** Our apartment building does, too.

Unit 14

We use **adverbs of manner** to show "in what way" actions happen. They often end in **-ly**.

Javier is singing loudly.

Here is how to form adverbs from adjectives:

quick → quickly   beautiful → beautifully   slow → slowly   easy → easily

Some adverbs are irregular:

good → **well**   fast → **fast**   hard → **hard**   so → **so**

Complete the sentences with adverbs.

1 He's a really good dancer. He dances _____________ (beautiful).

2 When she plays the piano, she moves her fingers _____________ (quick).

3 She reads every day. She can read _____________ (good).

4 We finished the test _____________ (easy).

Unit 15

Grammar: Adjectives with Prepositions

We use **adjectives** with **prepositions** to express people's feelings about something.

excited about the play

curious about the announcement

angry about the fight

sad about losing my homework

interested in cooking

bored with the movie

happy with the experiment

disappointed with the game

confused by the ending

surprised at his answer

Complete the sentences with the correct prepositions.

1 The sisters were happy _______________ their invention.
2 I was interested _______________ the story.
3 They were curious _______________ the principal's plans.
4 He was confused _______________ question.

Unit 16

Grammar: Polite Offers

We use **_Would you like ...?_** to make a polite offer. We use it to ask someone if they want to do something or want something. Follow **_Would you like ...?_** with *to* + verb or a noun.

Would you like to sit down?

Yes, I'd like to sit down. / Yes, I would.

Would you like some ice cream?

Yes, please. / No, thank you.

Unscramble the questions in your notebook.

1 like / Would / ? / another / you /peach
2 Would / ? / a pen / you / like / to borrow
3 to / try / like / Would / you / ? / the cookies
4 you / like / ? / a map of the museum / Would

Unit 17

Grammar: Prepositions of Movement

We use **prepositions of movement** to show which direction a person or thing is moving. Some prepositions of movement are: *into*, *out of*, *up*, *down*, *over*, *under*, *from*, *to*, *around*, and *through*.

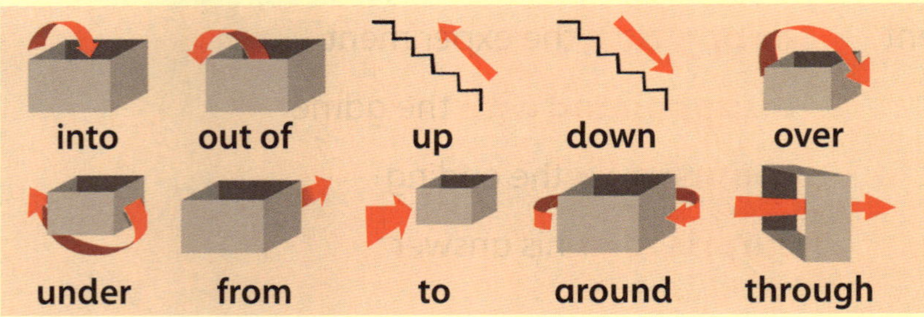

Complete the sentences with a preposition.

1 Can you put the groceries ________________ the refrigerator?

2 We went for a nice walk ________________ the lake.

3 To get there, you have to go ________________ the tunnel.

4 Oh, no! Our pet guinea pig climbed ________________ its cage!

Unit 18

Grammar: Want to, Need to, Have to

We use **want to** + verb when we are making a personal choice about an action.

Hakeem wants to play video games.

We use **need to** + verb or **have to** + verb when we don't have a choice about an action.

Hakeem needs to / has to do his homework first.

We use **want to** + verb, **need to** + verb, and **have to** + verb in the present tense or the past tense.

Hakeem wanted to ride his bike, but he needed to do his homework first.

He had to do his chores, too.

Circle the correct option.

1 I **want to** / **have to** go ice skating tomorrow.

2 We **want to** / **have to** turn off the lights when we don't use them.

3 They **needed to** / **wanted to** go skateboarding, but it was raining.

4 She didn't go to the movies because she **wanted to** / **had to** do homework.

Regular and Irregular Verbs

Regular Verbs

Most verbs are regular. Add **-ed** to form the past tense of regular verbs.

I was amaz**ed**.
We play**ed** games together.

Irregular Verbs

Some verbs are irregular and don't use **-ed** to form the past tense. Learn the past tense form of each verb. Below is a list of common irregular verbs.

Irregular Verbs

Base Verb	Simple Past	Base Verb	Simple Past	Base Verb	Simple Past
be	was, were	fly	flew	ride	rode
beat	beat	forget	forgot	ring	rang
become	became	freeze	froze	rise	rose
begin	began	get	got	run	ran
bend	bent	give	gave	say	said
bite	bit	go	went	see	saw
blow	blew	grow	grew	sell	sold
break	broke	hang	hung	send	sent
bring	brought	have	had	shut	shut
build	built	hear	heard	sing	sang
burn	burnt	hide	hid	sit	sat
buy	bought	hit	hit	sleep	slept
catch	caught	hold	held	speak	spoke
choose	chose	hurt	hurt	spend	spent
come	came	keep	kept	stand	stood
cost	cost	know	knew	swim	swam
cut	cut	lay	laid	take	took
dig	dug	lead	led	teach	taught
do	did	leave	left	tear	tore
draw	drew	let	let	tell	told
dream	dreamt	lie	lay	think	thought
drink	drank	lose	lost	throw	threw
drive	drove	make	made	understand	understood
eat	ate	mean	meant	wake	woke
fall	fell	meet	met	wear	wore
feel	felt	pay	paid	win	won
fight	fought	put	put	write	wrote
find	found	read	read		

Writing Process

Step 1: Brainstorm Ideas

- Write all the ideas that come into your mind.

- Don't stop to think about what you write. Just keep writing.

Step 2: Organize Your Ideas

- Put your ideas into groups. Each group will be a paragraph. Use charts and graphic organizers to help you.

- Think about how your ideas connect. What are the main ideas? Which details support that main idea?

- Decide what you want to say first, next, and last.

Step 3: Write a Paragraph

- Write your topic sentence first. This tells your reader what your paragraph is about.

- Write three or four sentences to support your topic sentence.

- Make sure all your sentences are about the main idea.

Step 4: Revise Your Work

- After you write your paragraphs, read them again.

- Are your topic sentences clear?

- Are your supporting sentences strong and in the correct order?

- Are your grammar and spelling correct?

Brainstorming and Organizing

Make charts like these to organize your ideas before writing.

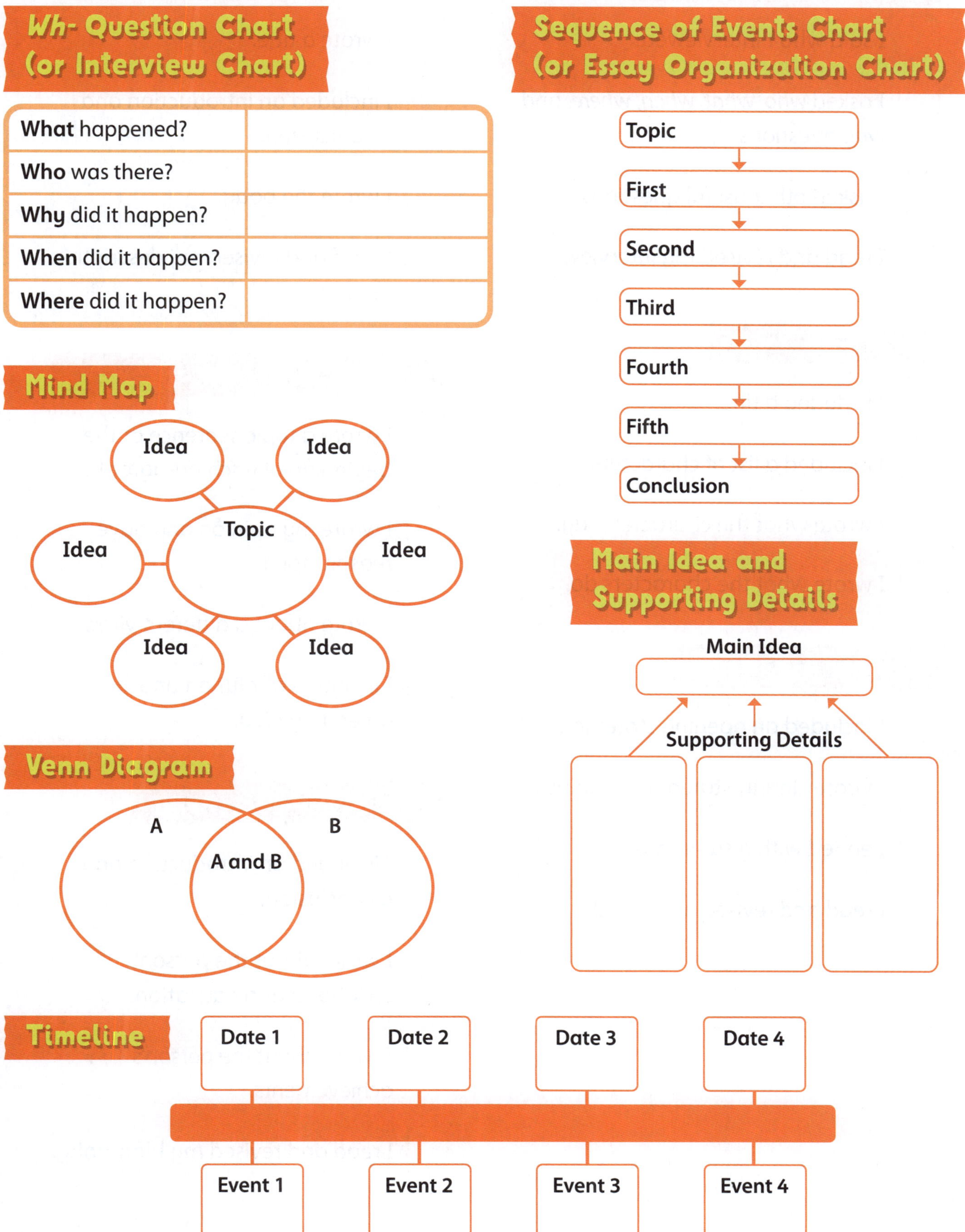

Writing Checklists

Unit 2: An Interview

- [ ] I said who I interviewed.
- [ ] I asked *who*, *what*, *when*, *where*, and *why* questions.
- [ ] I asked other useful questions.
- [ ] I read and revised my interview.

Unit 5: A Play

- [ ] I included a title.
- [ ] I included a list of characters.
- [ ] I wrote what the characters say.
- [ ] I wrote what the characters do.

Unit 8: A Speech

- [ ] I included an opening statement.
- [ ] I wrote clearly-stated main points.
- [ ] I ended with a summary.
- [ ] I read and revised my speech.

Unit 11: A Descriptive Text

- [ ] I wrote a title.
- [ ] I included an introduction and a conclusion.
- [ ] I wrote the body.
- [ ] I read and revised my descriptive text.

Unit 14: An Opinion Essay

- [ ] I wrote a topic sentence at the beginning of each paragraph.
- [ ] I wrote my opinion and gave reasons for it.
- [ ] I wrote about a different view.
- [ ] I included a solution and an ending idea.

Unit 17: A Biography

- [ ] I included an introduction and a conclusion.
- [ ] I wrote about the person's childhood and education.
- [ ] I wrote about the person's achievements.
- [ ] I read and revised my biography.